FROM PEOPLE PROBLEMS
TO PRODUCTIVITY

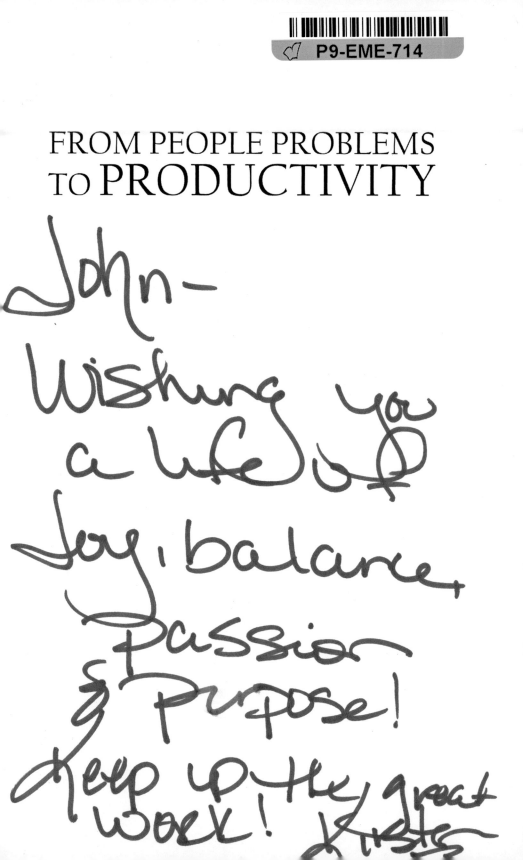

John —
Wishing you
a life of
Joy, balance,
passion
& purpose!
Keep up the great
work! Kristi

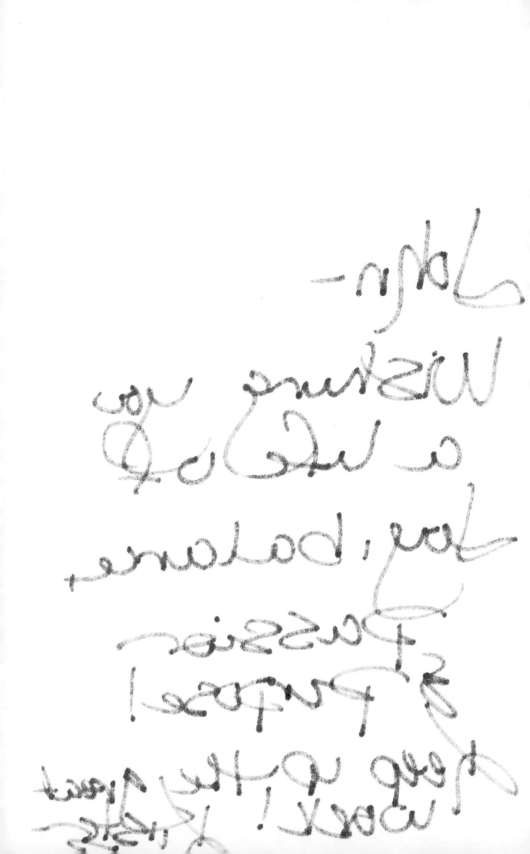

FROM PEOPLE PROBLEMS
TO PRODUCTIVITY
THE HEALTH PROFESSIONALS' GUIDE TO LEADING WELL

KIRSTEN E. ROSS, MLIR, SPHR

Outskirts Press, Inc.
Denver, Colorado

If you would like a downloadable version of the Catapult Tasks and forms
from this book, please visit http://www.FocusForwardCoaching.com and
click on the products page to purchase your copy. Use discount code
12577.

From People Problems to Productivity
The Health Professionals' Guide to Leading Well
All Rights Reserved.
Copyright © 2010 Kirsten E. Ross, MLIR, SPHR
V3.0

Outskirts Press, Inc.
http://www.outskirtspress.com

ISBN: 978-1-4327-6102-8

Outskirts Press and the "OP" logo are trademarks belonging to Outskirts Press, Inc.

PRINTED IN THE UNITED STATES OF AMERICA

Praise for the Process

"Kirsten Ross is an answer to prayer. As the Medical Director of a nonprofit Pediatric Medical and Rehabilitation Program that reaches out to Children with Disabilities and their families, there is a continual need to be not only a great physician, but a great organizational leader. The challenge of casting vision and "leading up" to hospital administrators, philanthropists, and societal leaders can be daunting.

Kirsten's skill in unveiling the 'best me,' allowing me to 'lead from the platform,' has me believing that I may just be able to take us there."

Dr. Susan Youngs

❦

"When I started with Kirsten I wasn't sure how she'd be able to help me and my business. In the first phone call I told her about several issues affecting my office and the moral in it. Over 6 months she helped me gain more confidence and empowered me to lead my employees and clinic better than ever before. As we changed to a more positive atmosphere the things she said would happen did. I now have a more positive clinic and have started to enjoy working in my clinic again with a new energy and empowered feeling. I would recommend Kirsten and her Drama Free Work Coaching to any employer."

Dr. Eric Lambert
Owner, Discover Chiropractic

"Before working with Kirsten, my voice was not heard. As a business owner, I had a difficult time with staff compliance and expectations. Through her practice building workshops and facilitated conversations we were able to come together as a team and I was able to become the team leader and boss I knew I always could be.

Dr. Rosemary Batanjski
Owner, Complete Care Chiropractic & Be Well in Birmingham

"If you have more than one person working in your office you need Kirsten! The improvement of communication and ease in the office is immediate. My personal challenge in communication was addressed and tailored to benefit myself with others in my working environment. It is a must for any physician desiring best patient care with office support and efficiency."

Dr. Featherstone
Owner, Universal Sciences Institute

"Kirsten's unique ability to clearly and quickly identify roadblocks to success and then provide powerful coaching to break down barriers has made a profound difference for McKinley. She is expert at guiding leaders through the most difficult and pervasive challenges. It is a testament to her abilities that she does so with the constant respect and gratitude of her clients, as well. We consider her to be

one of our most trusted advisors."

Karen Andrews
Chief Administrative Officer, McKinley & Assoc., Inc.

⚬◦◦⚬

"Kirsten is a wonderful coach and problem solver. Her ability to drill to the core of the matter is exceptional with excellent sugges-tions to work through the issues. Sessions with Kirsten will effec-tively improve all of your abilities to increase your productivity and communication."

Paul Redpath,
Vice President, TF Barry Co.

⚬◦◦⚬

"Kirsten has helped resolve many interoffice conflicts and tensions very quickly. The office runs smooth and more work gets done. She does a great job!."

Nicholas Tonkin,
Director of Corporate Wellness, Be Well and Owner, Engineered Athletics & Fitness

⚬◦◦⚬

"I had the pleasure to work with Kirsten my professional coach. She is able to core through the noise down to the key issues and guide you to clear decision-making processes. She is extremely effective in building teams and strong leaders. I hope to continue to know

Kirsten for years to come."

Karen Walworth,
Director of Marketing and Sales

ᔐᔑ

"Finding a great coach in the sea of coaches that are out there is a difficult task. Kirsten is one of those great ones. I cannot say enough about the wonderful work she has done with my clients. I get unsolicited rave reviews."

Gino Wickman,
Author of Traction: "Get A Grip On Your Business",
President at EOS Worldwide and creator of The Entrepreneurial Operating System (EOS)

Table of Contents

Forward - A Tale of Two Clinics

John wakes up before the sun, his wife and kids still asleep in their beds. Coffee mug in hand, he heads out with a peek and quiet kiss for his sleeping family. Their day won't start for another hour or so.

He makes the familiar drive to work, traffic on 115th, easy drive down Frazier St. and into the clinic. He is the first to arrive and unlocks the entrance for the employees.

Sitting at his desk John sips coffee and quietly completes patient charts as staff members begin to arrive. The quiet of the morning halts when he hears Linda and Barb complain about the new phone system as they take off their coats and settle in. It's going to be another one of those days.

As the morning continues, talk turns from frustration about the phones to frustration about patients and coworkers. John cringes when he hears his nurses grumble about a difficult patient; he rushes to the exam room so she won't hear the talk.

By afternoon, patients are stacking up and John is working through lunch. Hungry and depleted by the constant back and forth commentary and negative energy he heads to the front to see if Linda can hurry things along, "Everything okay up here?" he asks trying to swallow his building resentment. Barb turns with a list of complaints about the phone system and blames it for the delay. She even hung up on a few patients earlier, "Why can't you just go back to the old system?" "It was supposed to make things simpler," he thinks to himself. No sense saying it aloud. It would just invite more complaints. He slinks away silently to avoid the imminent confrontation.

As the last patient leaves, Linda rushes to lock the door behind him. Linda and Barb have now turned their criticism to another employee on vacation.

Did they even acknowledge the patient they just rushed out the door? He has been a patient for over 10 years and was just diagnosed with cancer. John storms into his office, fed up and overwhelmed. The stack of accumulated charts on his desk puts him over the top. This mess will have to wait until morning.

Do you see shades of yourself and your practice?

Organizational Stress

Health professionals and their employees are at a high risk of organizational stress. Working in an inefficient environment flooded with personal drama and employee complaints leads to high stress. The cycle perpetuates itself as more drama leads to higher stress.

Many clinics are plagued with this dynamic. It robs providers of their drive and siphons energy from the entire organization.

This book focuses on the negative dynamics and interactions that plague your clinic while giving you concrete steps to end the cycle of organization stress for yourself and your employees.

*What would your day look like
without these negative interactions?*

How much more effective would you be?

How many people could you help?

What if…

You woke up early, just like every morning. Sitting at your desk sifting through yesterday's charts you hear staff members starting to arrive. They laugh as they talk and you go to greet them, "Morning Ladies! How's everyone doing today?"

Once everyone arrives, you all meet in the break room. Linda, the receptionist, starts, "I thought Friday's patient flow went really well in the morning. Giving patients their paperwork ahead of time has made a big difference."

Sandy, the head nurse, agrees, "I think the patients noticed a difference too, that new approach seems to help a lot. What is on our plate today?"

Linda peeks at the schedule, "Well, Mrs. Johnson is coming in at 10:15 and we all know how difficult she can be."

Sandy has seen this before, "Yes, she can be difficult, but let's all remember she lives alone and is in pain much of the time. Remember, Linda, you will have some water waiting for her when she gets here and you know she likes it room temperature. Let me know when she arrives and I will take her back immediately. That usually seems to help move things along more smoothly with her. Everyone just keep in mind that she is experiencing a lot of pain and needs our support and everything should go fine! Does that sound good to you, Dr. Smith?"

"Absolutely, let me know when she arrives as well and I will poke my head in to say hi. Great huddle everyone!"

The new phone system starts making some trouble. Linda calls the help line to get technical assistance. She'll give you an update at the end of the day or during the morning huddle the following day.

The day charges on and exam rooms fill. You can hear Linda up front welcoming new patients and offering them some water. Patient charts are waiting at the door of each exam room when you arrive. By mid morning, Linda has finished reading the manual and has made a cheat-sheet for the phone system. Sandy sees her work and suggests she make a copy for everyone in the office, "This is great Linda!"

When Mrs. Johnson arrives, Linda is sure to remind the staff of how to handle her needs and odd requests. When the staff welcomes her, she immediately softens and waits in the exam room.

By 5:00pm, all exam rooms are empty and you have been able to finish up some charting while Linda and Sandy distribute the phone system cheat-sheets around the office.

"See you in the morning!" you shout from the parking lot just before heading home. It's been another successful day.

It is Possible!

Often when I first begin working with a clinic, the staff cannot visualize a day like the one described above. The clinic shown above is why health professionals started in their field. Unfortunately, many fail to experience it. Every one of them started out with a desire to heal and to serve. However, the reality of running this type of business quickly falls into this destructive cycle and the patients ultimately suffer.

The early stages of my process are always met with the usual responses, "It's always been like this." or, "This is just how it has to be. We are too busy."

Nevertheless, it is possible! I have been privileged to be an enthusiastic participant and witness to many clinics creating a new culture. Often the dramatic transformation happens within a few weeks. It takes an intentional focus and choosing to do what is necessary. However, it is possible and worth it!

Congratulations on taking the first step to moving your practice forward towards your original vision!

A Heart to Heal and Serve

In my 20 plus years of working with hundreds of health professionals, I have learned that you were born with a heart to heal and serve. You are built for compassion and empathy. You are wired with a passion to make others feel better.

Unfortunately, if you own your own clinic or hold a high-level leadership position in a larger health organization, you are faced with an internal struggle: that heart to heal gets in the way of the business side of your practice.

If you are like many of the Health Care Leaders I have worked with:

- You are overwhelmed, frustrated or resentful
- You work to exhaustion but feel like you never get anything done
- Your staff fail to follow-through no matter how many times you ask
- You feel misunderstood or unheard
- Your processes are falling apart
- You are failing to meet your income goals
- The constant focus on insurance companies, legislation and bureaucracy is zapping your energy and joy
- You have forgotten why you pursued this profession in the first place
- Your initial vision for your life seems nothing more than a memory now

My heart breaks when I meet a health professionals who have lost track of the passion that first pushed them towards their profession; are frustrated and overwhelmed with the red tape, staff and insurance companies and are ready to give up the fight.

You are a steward of your gift to heal others!
You help create miracles every day. With that
gift comes a duty to be the best you can be.

I wrote this book to help you bring back your passion, re-create your vision, re-focus your mission, and get your staff aligned with your work.

You can Create Real Change Now! This Book Will Help You to:

- Attach to Your Passion
- Create a Clear Mission & Vision for your Clinic
- Transform Your Leadership Style
- Create a Productive Team
- Minimize Malpractice Risk
- Increase Profits
- Consistently Integrate Effective Processes
- Delegate Well
- Hold Staff Accountable
- Communicate with Clarity
- Live Life from the Platform
- Eliminate Frustration, Defensiveness, Resentment, and Anger
- Add Energy and Passion back into Your Work and Life
- Decrease Drama

Introduction - How to Use this Book

This book is for Health Care Leaders who want a business that is on fire, not just with profits but also with heart. A business that is both efficient and effective.

You've tried multiple ways to improve the business and culture of your practice. You've worked to streamline and improve processes by implementing new phone systems, patient forms, marketing tools and more. Maybe you've even hired a process coach to come in and revamp your entire system.

No matter how much money you spend or how promising the improvement seemed, nothing has created lasting change. Staff resists new systems and even modest advancements revert to status quo within weeks.

So far, nothing has created the practice you desire. Nothing has left you feeling on fire, fulfilled, streamlined or effective.

As a result, you are disconnected from your passion and mission. The daily grind is zapping the energy and fire you once had for your work. These failed attempts have left you feeling disempowered in your own business, unable to make your vision a reality. Many professionals have given up.

My system can help you create the practice you desire. I want you to wake up excited to start your day and I want your staff to feel the same. My hope is for you to effortlessly create the important difference that you were meant to make. My goal is for you to know every day that you were given special gifts to use in service to others. You are a steward of these gifts. You are accountable to be the best you, the most focused you that you can be.

You can't run your practice alone, this book will give you the tools to train and hire your staff to work in alignment with your mission, goals, and vision.

Doesn't feel doable? Believe it or not, it is!!
And you now have the key to making it happen!

Book Sections

Eliminate Your Personal Barriers

This book has three main sections. In the first section, you will focus on identifying and removing your own personal barriers. You will determine what is keeping you from being fully wired for passion. You will also examine your current communication and delegation styles. In the process, you will become the kind of leader you need to be to make your vision a reality.

Engage Your Team

The second section will take you through what might be some of the most difficult as you evaluate your staff. However, you will also fire up your team to bring them on board to the new mission and culture. You will engage them in your vision. It is an exciting time of sharing!

Convene Your Remarkable Team

The third section is titled, "Convene Your Remarkable Team." During this section, you will be implementing the tools required to establish harmony and a successful culture. You will also be challenged to take action with employees who are having difficulty with change. In addition, we will also cover some useful hiring and retention strategies.

Tips for the Process

Let me tell you the secret that has led me to my goal:
my strength lies solely in my tenacity. ~ Louis Pasteur

Here are a few tips to use along with this program that will catapult your progress in creating your ideal practice.

Step One: Read to learn.

Take in information as a general concept. Do not get ahead of yourself by thinking about everything that is not working or must be changed. Take it one step at a time or you will become overwhelmed and discouraged. This book will help you make step-by-step methodical progress towards your goals.

Step Two: Focus on you and your practice.

It does you no good to focus on things outside your practice. If you begin to think, "Wow, 'ole so and so sure needs this. They should change this right away," you have stepped outside your area of control.

When your focus turns to others, you miss the opportunity to make change for yourself. Intentionally focus on how the information contained here can positively impact you and your practice. Period.

Too often, we use concern for others as a way to avoid our own shortcomings. So, yes, please do recommend the book to them but beyond that, drop it and consider your own circumstances. This book will prompt you to do some reality checking that may be difficult at times. When it does, just work to stay in it to get the most out of it for you!

Step Three: Attach the general concepts to your own life, work or experiences.

You create a deeper understanding when a new learning or thought process is attached to an old, well-known part of you or your life. Pay attention today and over time. Focus on continually applying the concepts learned here to your work and your life.

Discover things about yourself and your practice in the context of what you learn here. Create awareness about how the information can be applied to determine where you are doing well or where you need to place more emphasis. Be honest with yourself. During self-reflection, you will create a list of actions needed to move you and your practice forward.

Step Four: Take action!

As you go down the path of self-discovery or uncover areas in your practice that need attention, do not get overwhelmed and quit. Do not say, "There's just too much here. I will do it later." Later may never come. Today is the day.

You know as well as anyone that if you read a book or attend a conference, feel inspiration in the moment but then make no immediate change, the inspiration is gone and the ideas are lost. The book or notes sit on a shelf somewhere gathering dust.

Instead, get in action. Make the commitment to begin the step-by-step methodical process of change that is required. A journey begun whether long or short is better than a journey never started! You will get there. Like my dad always said about college at any age, "whether you go to college now or not, you'll still be 4 years older 4 years from now."

If you uncover many things that need to change do not let yourself feel overwhelmed. Instead, chunk it all down. To say it in another way, take the larger goals and break them into smaller tasks. Do not be concerned, there are exercises throughout the book to help you create a systematic plan to help you do just that.

Remember, you do not climb a mountain all at once. You do it one step at a time.

Step Five: Do the Catapult Tasks!

The exercises in this book are aptly named "Catapult Tasks". Completing them will catapult you towards the practice you desire. Reading without catapulting will be less effective. If you are taking the time to read then take the extra time to catapult! Knowledge about you or your business that you discover in each chapter will build in the next.

You may find it helpful to download the companion workbook located at http://www.FocusForwardCoaching.com. Visit the site and then click on the products page to purchase your copy. You can also sign up for your free newsletter.

Step Six: Commit to making intentional change.

Where you see opportunity for improvement in yourself or your practice, begin to take the methodical steps required to make the necessary changes. Change will not come overnight. Walking step by step through the Catapult Tasks will get you to your goal.

Step Seven: Stick with it!

Just do it. Keep walking it forward. Don't give up. Don't talk yourself out of it. Don't tell yourself it's good enough the way it is. Something inspired you to purchase the book. Some desire, some hope. Don't squelch it. You can do it!

The Importance of Commitment

Unless commitment is made,
there are only promises and hopes; but no plans
~ Peter F. Drucker

Throughout this book, you will see the word commit often. Use of this word is intentional. I will ask you to commit rather than to try. There are key differences between trying and committing.

We often are not aware of the language we use, what the words actually mean, or the power our words really have.

My book, *"Playing Life to Win"*, has a section on tentative language versus the language of action. This is the difference between words that water down our message and minimize our power versus words that communicate tenacity. **Commitment** communicates tenacity and a pledge towards action. **Try** communicates an attempt at action but tells nothing of to what degree. Try makes no promise of achievement.

To illustrate, hold your left hand up in the air. Now try to put it down. If you put it down, you did not follow the instructions. If you actually put your hand down, you are no longer trying. Trying is not accomplishing what you set out to do. Trying is just a promise to "give it a whirl", "give it a go", "I'll think about it", "I'll make an attempt". Trying says nothing.

Commitment is purposeful. It is a promise to achieve. You feel it. Communicating a commitment becomes a pledge to yourself or someone else. Committing to action is what will catapult you towards your goals. Trying gives no guarantee. This process will require you to commit rather than to try.

Commit for yourself, your patients, your staff, your family, your friends. Commit for those out there who could benefit from your work but don't know you yet. Commit for those you will provide services to through your charity work down the road. Commit for those who can benefit from your gifts. Commit to be a great steward of those gifts.

Here is your first Catapult Task. Will you pass it by or will you stop and take a moment to ponder and respond so that this information is cemented?

Catapult Task: Commit vs. Try

I see these areas in the past where I have *tried* but not *committed*:

I will drop the word try from my vocabulary. I commit to commitment.

Date & Sign

Catapult Task: Creating the Vision

If it all begins to feel too hard or overwhelming, like you would rather just limp along where you are because, hey, it's not that bad – take a quiet moment. Stop and think about each of these questions for a few minutes to get yourself on track. Really, experience what it would be like.

What would it be like to walk into your office and have an entire team there for a purpose, not just a paycheck?

What would it feel like to have your entire staff energized and fully engaged in helping your patients every moment of every day?

What would you feel like if the individual conflicts and drama became overshadowed by the bigger purpose of healing and health?

What would it feel like to focus the energy of every person on your staff towards one common purpose?

What would it look like to reclaim the time and energy lost to workplace drama and conflict?

What would it feel like to love your work again?

Take a moment to write about any additional thoughts:

One of the deepest innate human needs is to know that our lives count for something greater than ourselves. *Make your clinic the place where your staff members are fulfilling that desire.* This is exactly what wiring your practice for passion and profit can help you achieve!

- An energized and engaged staff
- Single-minded focus on healing
- Fulfillment and fun

Catapult Task: Motivation to Change

Some of us are motivated by punishment, others by reward. The first exercise is for those motivated by reward. Your motivation will come from working towards the big vision you have created for your business.

Others of you, however, are more apt to be personally motivated by avoiding negative consequences. In case the reward of achieving that great vision does not do it for you, we will do a second exercise to cover all of the bases.

It is time to really get at what it feels like to run your practice the way it is running now. Again, get at the experience, really feel it. The goal here is to paint a picture of the kind of experience you would like to avoid going forward.

Think of at least one time you experienced extreme frustration in your clinic. Maybe it was a high-drama day; you had poor patient flow or failing processes.

What happened?

Where were you when the situation was at its worst?

What did you say?

What did you do?

What did you think?

Who else was there?

How did you feel?

What did you tell friends or family – or did you just keep it to yourself?

What did you tell yourself about the experience afterwards?

How often is it like this now?

Take a moment to write about your experience:

Please keep these two Catapult Tasks close at hand. If you ever begin to feel like the work you are doing through this book is not worth it, re-read either or both to get back to why you are doing what you are doing. You know best which motivates you, moving away from the negative or moving powerfully towards the great.

Remember, you are a steward of your gifts. You need to be the best and most focused you possible. Your practice acts as an extension of you and your mission.

Section 1:
Eliminate Your Personal Barriers

*Leader of one, leader of many; if you can't
lead one you can't lead any. ~ Anonymous*

To be a great leader you must have vision, integrity, and tenacity. And you, my friend, must be a great leader! Even in a small practice, your staff is looking to you as a guide. You must have a plan and a purpose.

You cannot be a great leader if you have barriers getting in the way.

I love flying by the seat of my pants while on vacation. It is wonderful to get up with no plan and let the day unfold. You often find great adventure. However, in business, when others are relying on you for direction, you cannot operate like that.

In business you must lead with a blend of clarity for what gives you passion, a clear mission and vision to keep you aligned with that passion and the self-discipline and tenacity to stay in motion.

I use the analogy of a car:

- **Passion** is the fuel that will keep you moving through all seasons and around obstacles.

- **Mission and Vision** is the road map that tells you which way to go for the journey you are taking. You need this to stay on course.
- **Self Discipline and Tenacity** are your accelerators. You must take action; get in motion to make progress.

All Motivation, No Mission

Do you ever wake up in the morning get yourself together and rush out the door only to drive aimlessly in your car all day? No, of course not! But, this is what life looks like when you have tenacity and motivation but no clear road map.

You spent the entire day putting everything you had into something, and you never stopped to think about where you were going. It never occurred to you to pick a destination, let alone bring a map.

Hard work is required, but it accomplishes nothing if you do not know what you are working for. Running an office, or any business, without a clear mission and vision is like jumping in the car not knowing where you are going. All the energy, hard work, and strategy in the world will only leave you driving in circles. You must decide where you are going.

When you know your destination and you take the time to get a roadmap, the turns become obvious, forward progress can be measured, and goals are achieved.

So, this first section is all about you. You must first learn to lead yourself before you can lead others. The first step is to get you attached to your own personal passion.

How does it sound to be fully charged up and excited about your work again?

Next, you will walk through creating your clear mission and vision, the road map for your clinic.

The combination of fuel and direction will help you create the accelerators; give you the tenacity and self-discipline to catapult your progress. Do not worry if, at this point, you are saying you have no idea. The next steps will help you get there.

～⧉◎～

Find Your Passion Again

*There is no passion to be found playing small -
in settling for a life that is less than the one
you are capable of living. ~ Nelson Mandela*

I believe that we are all meant to live lives filled with joy and fulfillment; that we have gifts to be used in the service of others. Finding how to use those gifts and live a life of passion is our innate pursuit.

When you are wired for passion, you are focused on what is most important to you. You want to go to work everyday because you know you are making a difference. Decisions are made easily because you know what you want and what you do not. Petty distractions are a thing of the past because your purpose is bigger.

Passion is the fuel that pushes you through challenges, both real and imagined, and allows you to see the world as though anything is possible. It is being who you are meant to be and doing what comes naturally. It is like allowing water to gain velocity from its natural flow rather than trying to force it up and over a wall.

When you are attached to your passion, you know you are on the right track, which naturally provides the tenacity needed. You see only that which you seek to achieve! Tenacity drives you through the inevitable challenges.

When I'm working with clients, I often use the analogy of getting your screaming baby strapped into a car seat to illustrate tenacity. If you have kids, you have experienced tenacity! When you are putting your child in their car seat, your purpose is to make your baby safe. Your baby hates to feel confined and wants nothing to do with it. You cannot reason with a baby or explain your logic so you must just make it happen and there is nothing worse than hearing your baby scream. It's so difficult to hurdle the challenge of lovingly strapping them in as they arch away from the confinement and scream with all of their might. Your tenacity, however, dictates that the car will not move until the child is fully secure.

A strong purpose or passion without will or strong self-discipline gets you nowhere. You're like a race car in park with all the potential to move efficiently but you have no forward momentum.

On the other hand, strength of will without clear purpose and you are in constant motion seeking to achieve but in all different directions, more like a bumper car.

If I am wishy-washy about my desire to reach a goal because I lack the fire of passion I will be easily stopped by any challenge. I can tell myself that "It doesn't really matter", or, "This must be the sign that I am to work on something different." It's also easier to make excuses, "I just didn't have time for it" or, "Other things just seem more interesting."

Passion tells you that you are on the right track and keeps you moving towards what is possible.

That is the commitment level you want for your clinic. You shouldn't make a move, hire an employee, or add a service, unless it meets your mission, gives you passion. Passion gives you the fuel and the knowledge that you are on track.

What is driving your decisions now? Is it your unwavering focus on mission? Where are you letting those imagined obstacles like fear rob you of tenacity? Are you living your life as if you're floating on a lazy river, just bumping along with the flow of what's around you, or are you grabbing those paddles to accelerate and steer with all of your might?

If you do not have passion now, you did at one point. Something drove you through the education required for your profession. What was your driver then? You had obstacles and challenges but you did it. What gave you the tenacity to make it happen?

<u>Catapult Task:</u> Finding Your Original Passion

So, it is time to get reattached to the passion that brought you to this profession; time to get back to the basics. I know it is there. Few, if any, land in this profession by accident. It requires too much tenacity. You need to reattach to your passion and ambition before it was tainted with the realities of balancing work and family, running a business, and dealing with insurance companies.

Take the time to sit quietly, close your eyes and visualize. Again, really get into the entire experience so that you feel it, see it, taste it, smell it. Feel again that positive emotion of excitement, awe, appreciation, anticipation, or whatever it was for you.

Once you have it, experience it for a few moments and then take the time to capture the experience in words here. You will want to look back on this exercise when times get tough. It will help pull you back to your positive and heartfelt experience. This is the reason you do what you do.

Where were you when you first felt a tug for your profession?

Whom did you first talk to about it?

What did you say?

How did you feel?

What barriers did you identify that you were afraid might stop you?

Where did you show tenacity in getting to where you got?

What was your big vision then?

What did you think it would be like?

What was your hope for the future?

What did you think when you decided to be in the profession - your big ideas - what changes did you plan to make in the world with your gifts?

Take some time to write any additional thoughts:

Now, visualize the first time you helped heal someone. Or, perhaps there is a time when you helped to create a dramatic difference in someone's life that really stands out. Recall as many details as you can. Even if you are not routinely involved in direct patient care you have played a role many times:

Where were you?

What was their first name?

What was the issue?

What did you do?

Who else was there?

How did the patient respond?

How did friends and family respond?

What color was the room?

What did you do right after?

What did you tell others about the experience?

What did you feel?

What vision did you create that day for your future in this profession?

What was your hope for your future?

This is why you do what you do, isn't it?

ᴄ∕ᴏ ᴄ∿

Scanning for Additional Clues to Your Passion

Now let's scan the years since to look for additional clues to your passion. That original passion might need clarifying or transformation.

Feeling a Call to Action

When in your life have you felt a call to action? Maybe you actually did something, started on a new mission, wrote a letter, thought about getting involved, or maybe you just sat on your hands and did nothing. I bet you remember. It is probably one of those defining moments.

I am talking about those times in your life when you felt this big tug at your heart. Or, perhaps thoughts raced through your head. Things like, "How can something like this be happening?" "Something has got to be done about this!" The heart zings, the tugs when you are doing your work give hints that you are on the right path. Other calls may happen in areas where you are not currently focusing. It is that nagging feeling that "I can not stand that this exists."

It's okay if you did nothing at the time. The question is not meant to criticize. The goal here is to look for world issues that move you. And the "world issue" might be in your next-door neighbor's house. It does not have to be a big grand thing. Big or small, these events will give you clues to where your heart feels a tug. Tugs at the heart will help you find your passion.

So, think back. When have you felt a call to action? Maybe it was;

- a commercial on television,
- a program,
- an event,
- a conversation

Heart's Desire

I had the opportunity to hear Beth Moore speak and for several hours, she taught about the concept of, "your heart's desire" and, "the desires of your heart". According to her message, God puts a desire on our hearts. It will stand the test of time and circumstance. Sometimes we squelch the desire. It can become too painful if we are unable to see a clear path to that desire. Or, perhaps you've tried and have been unsuccessful so you just stored it away. Regardless of why the heart's desire is squelched, it always remains ready to be tapped.

If you do not know what your heart's desire is, it can be helpful to look at any jealousies you experience. Is there a pattern? Of course I am not talking about jealousy over material possessions. We can feel big pangs of jealousy when others have achieved what our heart desires. Jealousy is not a good emotion, but it will give you useful information.

If you can bring your heart's desire into your awareness, it is another method to help you find your passion and purpose.

Catapult Task: **Calls to Action and Heart's Desires**

Take a minute to capture any recollections you had about calls to action you have felt in the past:

Where have you experienced jealousy over another person's accomplishments?

What other clues can you conjure about your heat's desires?

∽∾∾

At this point, you may be very clear on your passion and mission. It was just a matter of picking it back up and dusting it off. Others may need more clarifying work. Either way, it's okay.

Now that you are aware and looking, you will begin to see clues that would have gone unnoticed before. Finding your sweet spot, your specific passion and mission can take time. Give yourself grace. You can always hone and modify as you go. Don't let the bit of unknown or uncertainty stop you in your tracks. Take what you have gleaned so far during the chapter and see that as a starting point. I speak from personal experience and from the experience of many of my clients; once you get intentional you begin a path that leads you closer and closer to your purpose. So, don't stop now. Congratulate yourself for the progress you've made so far and keep moving forward!

⟡

Create a Clear Business Mission & Vision

The very essence of leadership is that you have to have vision. You can't blow an uncertain trumpet.
- Theodore M. Hesburgh

You have found your passion, or are on your way. Now you must put it to work in your clinic. As the leader of your organization, your staff is looking to you for direction, guidance, and purpose. You have hired them; it is up to you to communicate for what purpose.

It is time to put that vision and passion into words and actions that communicate to others what you would like to accomplish and how they can be a part of it. Remember, this will become your road map.

Step 1 to creating a passionate focus for yourself and your staff is to develop your Mission Statement for your practice. A mission statement describes the purpose of your organization, the common goal that all employees are focused on achieving every day.

The book "Be Unreasonable" says, "When you are simply following things that seem like good ideas, you are apt to abandon them if you meet obstacles. The idea that once seemed so attractive is not at all enticing when the going gets tough. However, when you and your team are focused on a specific mission, everyone is more motivated to take risks, get in action, and look beyond the obvious."

The mission statement you develop should get your blood flowing. It should make you want to stand up and fight for your cause. To successfully implement your mission it must be strong enough to keep you motivated. Motivation is only 20% cerebral and 80% emotional. You are relying on emotion to keep this train moving down the tracks.

While the emotion, the passion, is what drives you to keep at your goals, you must combine that passion with expertise. Emotion alone does not get you very far.

At a minimum, your mission should:

- Communicate the purpose of your organization both internally and to the community.
- Establish a framework for strategic planning and business development
- Include measurable and concrete objectives
- Evoke emotion
- Motivate those involved with your organization to work towards the goals you have established

If you already have a mission statement, pull it out, dust it off and look it over. Did you create one to meet requirements of some insurance company or governing board or did you write it for you? How strong is it? Are they just words on a page or does it evoke emotion? Does it reflect the goals you established earlier; does it reflect your passion? The work you've completed in the last chapter may inspire you to re-think your mission statement. It may need a tweak or an entire makeover.

Catapult Task: **Creating Your Passion-Inspired Mission Statement**

Take a moment to fill in the blanks, either from your current mission statement or starting from scratch. This Catapult Task will help you clarify and verbalize the goals that have you fired-up.

- What unique purpose does your clinic or organization serve to patients?
- What unique purpose does it serve to the community and its employees?
- How would you like to use your own talents in the world?
- Your organization was started to fill a void in the marketplace, either to provide something new or to improve upon services already offered through the competition. What void does your organization fill in the marketplace?

The unique purpose of my organization is:

We provide _____ to our patients.

We provide _____ to our employees.

We provide _____ to our community.

Who are you in business to serve? Just as the pediatrician could easily pass up the opportunity to buy a machine for elderly patients, by defining your target demographic, you can easily begin to tailor your growth to meet the needs of your target market. If you do not have a clear idea of whom you are serving, think of the last patient who saw significant improvement and whom you felt you had an impact on. If you see a pattern, it might show you the types of patients you should focus on.

We are here to serve:

- How does your organization seek to serve the population you described above?
- Consider the services offered. At what stage in an illness or recovery do patients come to your office?
- What need of those individuals does your organization serve?

We serve our patients by:

- What public image would you like your organization to reflect?
- Is your organization academic in nature, fun-loving and free-spirited, child-friendly, or a safe environment focused on healing?
- What perception do you want to convey when someone reads your mission statement?

Our public image is:

What role does your staff play in moving the organization towards its goals?

The mission statement should serve as a guide for each staff member when he or she makes a decision that affects the company. Consider the role you believe the staff plays in the everyday advancement of your mission. Are they partners in caring for patients, or do they maintain the profitability of the clinic to keep the doors open? To motivate staff with the mission statement, they must have a clear vision of how they fit into the picture.

Our staff progresses our mission by:

As you look over your answers to the above questions, think of ways to put these pieces together that concisely communicate these points in an emotional way.

Our Mission is:

Don't focus on getting the mission perfect the first time, focus on getting the right objectives in place. At this point, make sure the goals described are those that you are most passionate about and feel your organization can best affect. There is no right answer, only the one you are most excited about. Your mission statement is about your personal definition of success and how you feel the talents of your organization can be used to best affect those you are passionate about serving.

Take a few minutes to look over the mission statement you have written,

- Is it concise?
- Is it a strong statement?
- Does it evoke emotion?
- Is it accurate?
- Is it complete?
- Does it establish concrete objectives?
- Could it be used to guide business decisions?

When you are happy with the mission you have developed, ask for feedback from colleagues and team members. Feedback from others can be helpful at all stages of the development process. Other members of the organization will have different views of its impact and importance to the community and to patients. Incorporating multiple points of view can help shape your mission into a comprehensive vision that includes every member of your staff.

Strong Mission, Strong Organization

The mission statement that you have developed should be displayed prominently throughout the office. Each employee should know the mission of the organization as well as his or her role in that mission. All organizations benefit from a strong mission statement that provides the focus described earlier. Once everyone begins working towards the same goal, business decisions about day-to-day operations, task distribution, accountability, and staff interaction all become easier.

For example, a clinic has established providing health care services and education for the underprivileged as its focus and objective. This clinic may want to consider delegating the task of gathering education materials to a specific staff member. Before, this task may have been a side issue preformed by various employees. Additionally, if the state begins offering seminars for health care providers and their staff about the new laws associated with Medicaid, taking a retreat day for the team to attend would further the goals of the clinic.

Without clear objectives, these two decisions may be seen as frivolous or wasteful. The new objectives would also quickly show that the staff should not invest large amounts of time or money into a seminar for cosmetic surgery, as this would probably not advance the goals of the clinic.

Catapult Task: Aligning with Your Mission

Now that you have put a lot of thought into your mission and why you go to work every day, consider how well the day-to-day operation of your clinic currently supports this mission. Don't get discouraged by this. If your clinic fully supported your mission there would be no problems and you would not be reading this book. And, I guarantee, you are not alone.

Chances are you will find many areas where your clinic is not living up its potential. No worries! You are on the right path now. And, next, I'm going to show you how to get into action fixing what you uncover.

First, we are going to take your mission apart, piece by piece.

Write out the first major goal, objective, or description in your mission statement.

- **Is this an accurate description of your clinic?**

- **Do you currently work towards this goal?**

- **Could you put more energy behind this and make it a greater part of your clinic?**

- **The first part of your mission statement is important; you put it first for a reason. Is this the primary focus or image of your clinic?**

Write down your thoughts on how your clinic measures up to this standard.

Go line-by-line and word by word through your mission statement and pinpoint those areas that you feel your clinic is currently strong in and which areas your clinic might be weak.

My clinic fulfills my Mission Statement in the following areas:

My clinic falls short of my Mission Statement in the following areas:

You should celebrate the areas you have identified as strong! Let your staff know what they are doing today that is fulfilling your mission. Tell them directly how they are succeeding. Take the time to understand how well you are already doing. And, you are already doing so many things right! Pat yourself on the back!

Now, where there is opportunity for improvement don't beat yourself up or have a pity party. And certainly, DO NOT QUIT! You have important work to do in this world. Just keep taking it one step at a time and stay in action knowing that you are moving forward now!

Later you will also be using this information to create some short and long-term goals.

⸙

Maintain a Laser Focus

The sun's energy warms the world. But when you focus it through a magnifying glass it can start a fire. Focus is so powerful! ~ Alan Pariser

Without looking, think quickly about how many light fixtures are in the room right now? What color is the car that you are parked next to?

Your brain noticed. But the information was not stored for ready access. You had not trained your brain or requested it to take in that information and store it.

We are bombarded with stimuli twenty-four hours per day, seven days per week. We get stimulus through our eyes, our ears, even our skin. To be efficient our brains take in only what we have deemed important or relevant. This information is what I call, "being on your radar screen." Other information is not registered for easy access.

So, an example would be deciding to buy a specific kind of car. Prior to thinking about this purchase, you probably never really noticed any on the road. However, as soon as you make the decision or even begin to ponder purchasing it, you will see them EVERYWHERE! Did thousands of people spontaneously decide to buy the same car at the same time? NO! You made the car relevant by beginning to think about it. Your decision to make it relevant put the car on your radar screen. Your brain was now triggered to take in that piece of information in as important and register it. Bingo! You now notice the car.

When I do my presentation, "Designing a Drama Free Workplace", I have the participants stop at this point and notice all of the things in the room that were previously NOT on their radar screen. It's a great exercise to help you realize how much you are missing in each moment. Why don't you stop reading for a minute and just do the exercise where you sit.

- Begin to notice the noises that you had just left in the background. Is there air conditioning or heat running? Or maybe you are in a park and there is a din of cricket sounds, frogs, buzzing bees, or birds. Is there traffic noise?
- Look around you at the floor or ground, the bench or chair

you are sitting on, the walls or trees, the ceiling or sky. Are there stains, clouds, bugs, paint chips, flowers that had previously escaped your notice? What pieces of information do you pick up as you intentionally choose to aim your focus in a new direction?

- What are you sitting on? How does your body feel pressed against it? How do your feet feel where they touch the floor or ground? How does your arm feel as it rests on your thigh, the pillow or arm of the chair? How do your feet feel inside your shoes?

All of this information is stimulus that your brain could have readily registered but chose not to according to your current focus.

Every little item that you notice now was a possible nugget of information to take in and store. Can you imagine what would happen if we were bombarded with every piece of information coming at us all day everyday? Our brains are miraculous and I am simplifying the topic tremendously!

Now, I am talking about your brain like it is a separate entity. And, in some ways, it is. It does function without our conscious effort in many ways but we are the ultimate master. We get to control much of the work that our brains do. For instance, we are able to hold our breath for a period, even though our innate functioning will not allow us to hold it until we die.

And there is a primal part of our brain that registers danger and fear out of anything novel. It is meant to act as an efficient diagnostic center to help us avoid negative circumstances in our environment. Unfortunately, it is usually calibrated too high and considers anything new and different as a threat. This part of our brain is on autopilot as well. We cannot turn it off. However, we can control how we react to the thoughts of pending doom and fear. We can be stopped in our tracks or we can do some reality checking and then bust through that fear and keep going anyway.

Likewise, we can take intentional control of what our brains deem important or relevant so that we are in charge of what data is registered and which is ignored. This is why creating a laser mission and vision for your business is so important. Now that you have established your succinct, passion-emoting statements of purpose, (and my hope is that you have completed that step before getting here), your brain will look for all data relevant to meeting your mission. Any opportunity that will move you towards your mission will come into focus and be stored as relevant. Your brain will hone in on tidbits of information that otherwise could have been missed.

This is why focusing on your clear mission and vision is so important. Phase 1 is creating it. Now you must keep your focus there.

Without a mission and vision giving you a road map, you cannot create intentional, laser focus. The target is too large and scattered. Your brain will pick up random opportunities in a scattered pattern. You can't move forward on the straight path that you achieve with a refined focus.

Picture a dartboard. Without a focus on mission and a vision, the entire board is your target. You might pick up a piece of equipment from the lower left side and then hire a staff member who meets criteria from the top right. Your marketing materials might be designed for top left. They will not be a perfect match.

On the other hand, with a clear focus, you hone in on the bullseye alone. Staff members, equipment, marketing materials, your clinic environment, patient education, the services you provide, and the equipment you purchase are all aligned to hit that one center target.

I once had a client who had a written mission statement but hadn't looked at it in years. We revisited it together. In it, he had clearly stated that a focus for his practice was to care for children. I asked him to go look at his waiting room. It was near the end of the day so there were just two elderly patients sitting there. It was a beautiful room with fancy chairs and artwork on the walls. A table was lined with magazines in an orderly curl: Time, Sports Illustrated, Fortune, and O Magazine.

We then pulled out his drawer of patient education materials. It was all geared towards adult patients.

I asked him to look at how his staff members dressed. They all looked great. He had managed to maintain a high standard for the dress code. But all were in solid, muted colors.

There was nothing in that place that called to a child. Actually, as a mom, that waiting room would have been a heart attack waiting to happen. I kept thinking about how stressful it would be to contain two boys where they couldn't touch anything; there was nothing there to engage them during a wait. I would not have wanted to bring my children there and neither would any other parent.

I had to stop and ask him whether this really was his mission and vision for his practice. Did we need to do some revamping of the statements or some revamping of the office?

To him it was a no-brainer. He still felt a strong call to action to care for children. He had been feeling frustrated as his patient base got older and older and hadn't ever taken the time to connect the dots.

All it took was a few minutes with the mission statement and he was back on track fully focused and attached to his original passion. Now there was a specific target to move powerfully towards.

Within a few weeks he and his staff had changed some wall colors, added some puzzles and an activity corner to the waiting room that included a beautiful little aquarium, modified the dress code to patterned scrubs to infuse some fun, added some wall activities to two of the patient rooms, purchased some kids book and, of course, Highlights Magazines.

The staff also began encouraging current patients to bring their children in for a checkup. Most had never considered the idea. But with the new look and feel and the suggestion from the staff, soon there were children. The Dr. was reignited with passion and his practice grew immediately as current patients brought family members.

The mission and vision existed but he had gotten off track. He will now keep intentional focus on the bullseye. He was lucky; it was not too difficult to get back on target and often that is the case. However, you will not spontaneously get there. You have to utilize good focus to keep your actions aligned with your mission.

With intentional laser focus, you will put all of your cognitive energy powerfully towards the result you desire.

Honing Your Focus Further

So, you're sold on the idea of focusing in on your mission. Now let's hone the intentional focus further. Because even once you have a clear understanding about where your mission is taking you, you can still lose focus. In the equation of "getting what I want" or "reaching my goals", there are two main variables: things that help me get to where I want to go and things that stand in my way.

As we have demonstrated through our activities in the last section, in every moment of every day there will be a wide variety of things to focus on. In each moment, there will be the opportunity to focus on things standing in your way or things moving you forward. Which will you choose?

I still remember a couple of years ago being at a regional meeting for the Michigan Chiropractic Association in Royal Oak, Michigan. One of the doctors stood up at the end of the meeting and talked about how down he had been. He had gotten to a point where he felt like just giving up. He kept battling with insurance companies to get paid for his work; his employees were driving him crazy. His whole focus was on the negative in his practice. My heart broke for him as he spoke. His full focus had transitioned to all of the barriers to doing the work he had once loved.

Then he told the story of experiencing a turning point. A patient came in who had not been able to use his arms for 10 years. Through several months of treatments, he was able to give the man use of his arms again. The man had even been able to golf – he began to fill the room with energy as he told the story of how his focus had turned.

This Chiropractor was once again focused on his passion and had moved away from focusing on things in his way. That positive perspective was there all along. It was just a matter of shifting his focal point. It was so inspiring!

Any of us can get to where this Chiropractor was at his lowest point if we aren't careful. Life is not without challenge. Focusing on what stands in your way will put your brain on overdrive looking for more things relevant to what is standing in your way. You will begin to feel bombarded by issues, problems, roadblocks, and barriers. It's hard to keep your momentum when you are plagued by things in your way. I know there are many frustrations dealing with insurance companies, processes not working well, patients who miss appointments, staff not following your lead. There are plenty of options for you to focus on here if you choose.

So, rather than focusing on "things in your way," it is important to stay focused on things that help you get what you want. You are led by your focus. Won't life be more enjoyable if you are constantly looking for things that help you get your way? What opportunities will you notice that you might have otherwise missed?

Anthony Robbins tells a great personal story to illustrate the point. Anthony, a well-known motivational speaker who seems to live quite an adventurous life, decided to learn to drive a racecar. One of the first main concepts that he was taught was that where you look while you are driving is where the car will go – fast! Under these circumstances, it became necessary to get this focus point down immediately, for survival!

Coming into a turn, what is your greatest fear? Hitting the wall! Where did Tony look? At the wall! Where did the car go? At the wall!

Luckily, he had the help of an instructor sitting next to him who could grab his head and physically move it to make him re-focus back down the track. As soon as he looked down the track, as if by magic, the car began to go down the track and away from the wall. Phew!

Our lives work the same. We steer towards what we put our focus on. Only we don't have an instructor sitting next to us to re-position us. That's why I emphasize so strongly the importance of "intentional" focus. We need to be our own instructor. Even if you hire a coach who is helping you stay focused week to week, you don't have an instructor with you 24/7. You need to create the tenacity to maintain focus while your brain and those around you try to focus you elsewhere.

Focus on the progress you are making and what you need to do next, not on all that you have left to do. Focusing on the entire scope of your mission will leave you feeling overwhelmed and depleted. It's easy to talk yourself into giving up. It can feel safer and easier to stay put. You need to follow the lead of the successful mountain climber. They cannot think about every step, every crevice, and every challenge to be faced on the way up. They must give full, laser-focused attention to the current step, the current challenge. To do anything else can spell disaster.

Focus on you and what you want. Or, if you believe in a higher power of some sort, on what your maker has designed for you. Your parents, other family members, friends and colleagues all mean well when they share advice or give their opinion. And it is fine to consider their input. But do not put your focus here. If you allow the input from too many sources into your life's direction you will feel frustrated and uncertain. Everyone will have a different opinion, whether based on fact or not. Everyone will have a different perspective. No one will have the complete perspective that you used to create your own direction.

If you've had children, you know the experience of picking out a name for your baby. How many of you made the mistake of telling people the names you were considering before your little one was born? Before it is official, everyone feels entitled to share his or her opinion about the name. Some will like it, some will not. If you listened to all of the opinions, the birth certificate probably stayed blank for a while.

If, however, you took the safer route of keeping the name secret until the baby was born and so-named, you deal with none of that. Once the name is attached to your bouncing bundle of joy there is no thought of whether it is right; it just is.

Your journey to your mission is the same. Along the path, many will feel a need to provide their two cents. Once there, however, there is nothing to do but congratulate. The surest path is with the fewest critics. Secure your own focus by allowing only some a voice.

Trusted advisors are, however, another story. You want input from knowledgeable individuals. Advisors must be hand-selected for their wisdom, their passion for your mission, and their ability to exhibit self-control. You want people who will stop offering advice and respect your decision once you say that it is final. Seek out advisors who are not interested in pushing their own agenda or being right, who will not be defensive if you choose against their best judgment. It is a true gift when you find someone who provides well-thought out advice and affords you the freedom to do with it what you will.

Avoid The Bright Shiny Object Syndrome

Every time you go to a convention or even your local monthly association meeting or read a journal, you are bombarded with information about new technologies or equipment, new processes, the latest and greatest script or marketing idea. It is great to learn and stay up-to-date on the latest and greatest in your field but there is never a requirement to purchase, implement, or to make changes based on every new idea.

Without a clear mission, it is sometimes difficult to determine if you should participate in the next new thing.

I call this the Bright, Shiny Object Syndrome. It's easy to get distracted by something that shows potential for your practice, but you are a limited resource. You must limit your focus to those things that bring you closer to your mission. Period.

Implementing the next new something takes your focus away from other things. It must. I do believe that you can create more energy, which we will discuss later. But you cannot create more time. Once you have a clear mission, deciding whether to take on the next new thing is a very simple task. It boils down to a simple yes or no question that you should be asking yourself all day, everyday. Write it down and keep it handy.

Does this help me meet my mission?

Yes = Go

No = Stop

Simple! But as with most things, it's harder to do in real life.

To help illustrate the point further, here is a form I have my clients fill out. Sometimes seeing the reality helps make it more concrete. We move out of denial.

<u>Catapult Task:</u> Saying Yes – Saying No

By saying YES to:

I am saying NO to:

By saying YES to:

I am saying NO to:

By saying YES to:

I am saying NO to:

⚬๑⚬

Communicating Healthy Boundaries through the Art of "No"

Speaking of saying yes and saying no, have you learned to say both effectively? Learning to say no is a required skill if you are going to work efficiently towards your goals. If you do not say it enough you will never have control of your time. Others *WILL* monopolize you. And, if all of your time is taken in pursuit of other people's agendas you will have no time for your own important mission.

If you have become the go to gal or guy who never says no that is very convenient for the people in your life, but how is it working for you? As I have said before, you can create more energy but you cannot make more time. So, you can only add so much and if you can't say no you will be overwhelmed. Moreover, if you are to the point of being overwhelmed you are also carrying resentments towards many of the people in your life. You think they should know that you have too much going on. Well, they don't! Unless your life is filled with an unusual number of mind readers, they are not going to know unless you open your mouth and speak the words.

So, saying "No" is an important skill. If you have an issue with saying no you need to work on it. I often find that my clients do better with change when they figure out WHY they are doing something. When you know the why and see that it lacks validity there's your motivation. So, let's take a look at some of the key reasons many of my clients have given for failing to use the word no appropriately. Do you see yourself in any of these descriptions?

- **Guilt:** You feel bad if you say no. People need your help. The truth is, maybe if you said no they would have some other resources to tap, or they'd figure out another way, or do it themselves. It might even provide them with a growth opportunity as they stretch themselves to achieve something without you.

- **You want people to like you:** You think doing things for others will require them to like you and if you say no they will not. If this is you, it probably is true about the people in your life because you have become a magnet to people who base their relationships on what others can do for them. The truth is that people who really care about you for you will like you regardless of what you *do* for them. Your relationships will become richer.

- **You need to feel useful:** If you are not doing for others, where is your value? This is a rough way to live. Your self-esteem and self-worth are based on others appreciating your selfless acts. Your entire focus is on finding people to assist. There is no room or time for focus on you or your own mission as you search for your next fix. And, at times, the people in your life are not appreciative of the work you've done.

Then what?

- **You believe it is selfish to say no:** You believe that everyone else's needs are more important than your own and that self-sacrifice is virtuous. All of your time and energy is spent on others. You place no value on your own wants, needs or pursuits. This begs the question, "if you do not place any value on your needs and pursuits, then who will?"

So, do you see yourself in any of these descriptions? Did you have any "aha" moments"

Catapult Task: Can You Say No?

I use these excuses to avoid saying no:

How are these beliefs false?

What impact does this belief have on you, your practice, your life?

❧ ❧

Tips to Help you Say No

If you are new to saying "no," it can be difficult at first. Here are some quick strategies that you can implement immediately to assist you as you work that muscle.

- **Buy Yourself Time:** Practice using some of these statements to give yourself time. You should be doing some checking before you make that next big commitment anyway. The key is to make sure that you actually follow through with an answer, though. Do not use the delay as an excuse to avoid answering altogether. That is passive behavior and you do not want that.

  o Let me check my calendar,
  o I'll get back to you in a couple of days,
  o Let me think about that,
  o I need to check with my husband, wife, significant other, kids' calendar, business partner

- **Create Policy Statements:** Policy statements sound official and take the pressure off of you. It makes it appear as though the decision is cast in stone and is completely out of your hands. And you need some policy statements to stay on mission anyway.

  o I have a policy not to volunteer in the evenings.
  o We have committed to doing no more than 5 hours per month and we've already hit our quota for the month.

o I have already committed my budgeted dollars for the month.

- **Shift the Focus:** People making the request have a full focus on themselves. Shift the focus elsewhere using good eye contact and empathy for their situation. To do otherwise makes you appear guilty.

  o This is not about you, I need to say no for me.
  o I am sorry for your situation but my patients are my only focus right now.

- **Know Your Priorities:** Know your priorities ahead of time so that you can stick to them. If, for instance, you set a priority of the family eating together, then you must say no to all intrusions. If you must spend extra time in your clinic for the next two months know that and state it.

  o I'm sorry. I need to say no this time.
  o My number one focus is on (name the priority) right now. I can't this time.
  o If it is a boss giving you more work than you can handle, go to them and ask, "Can you please help me prioritize? I have all of this on my plate. What would you like me to put on hold?" Or, "How would you like me to prioritize this new work?"

- **Keep It Simple:** No long-winded explanation or excuses. This just makes you sound defensive. Practice stating your case and then stop. Continue to use good eye contact.

  o I'm sorry, I can't.

    o   I won't be able to this time.

- **Tackle Easy Situations First:** Start by saying no to the paperboy or the phone solicitor first. Build the muscle on the easy ones and then tackle your overbearing relative.

Below is one of my favorite quotes! Sometimes when we first begin to speak up we are fearful. That can make your voice shake. But, who cares? Speak up anyway. It gets easier and easier! You will be saying no with finesse before you know it.

"Speak Your Mind, Even if Your Voice Shakes."
Maggie Kuhn, social activist, 1905-1995

✑✑

Design a Business and a Life

How am I going to live today in order to create the tomorrow I'm committed to? ~Anthony Robbins

I believe strongly that, if you are a business owner, it is not just about designing a business. You also want to design a life.

Have you ever heard of a plant called the Passion Fruit? Its beautiful blooms are called Purple Passion. This plant and its flowers are well named. It grows without boundaries. Once planted, if left to its own devices, it will take over everything else around it. It will grow up trees, overtake other plants, and climb the exterior walls of your home. It is a completely unruly plant and provides the perfect analogy of passion unchecked. It provides beautiful flowers but it refuses to grow within confines and has the power to consume an adjacent area seemingly overnight. So, do we want passion in our lives? Yes! But we need to create some boundaries to keep it in balance.

Passion that overshadows every other aspect of your life can leave you feeling resentful, overwhelmed and with a lot of issues in your primary relationships. In other words, far from joy! And, I hope that this book unleashes your passion in a way that allows you to feel joy to new heights. But you cannot let your passion usurp every other aspect of your life.

On the path to meeting your mission, you will want to create some measure of success that includes timelines. Setting deadlines for key milestones will help you keep moving forward with intensity. It is important to be intentional when you set deadlines. If you overstate what is possible you will be frustrated as you fall short of your goals. Understate and you will be lollygagging along with little progress. This too can lead to frustration. These timelines will help you set expectations for yourself and your staff.

You must create space for family, friends, your physical health, your spiritual endeavors and personal growth in addition to your professional pursuits. If you don't, you will actually have less energy to put towards your mission and more chance of feeling burned out and overwhelmed. Laser focus does not mean all-encompassing focus for all time.

In the book, *The Power of Full Engagement*, the authors teach the concept of managing energy rather than time. It is their assertion, and I agree, that intentional choice that allows us to fully participate in each area of our lives provides more energy overall. Neglecting some major life areas will actually lower energy and decrease your effectiveness.

We are meant to live lives filled with passion and joy. So, let's set your timelines in a way that allows you to be energized and celebrate successes often!

You can fit most of your life activities into six main categories. To live a fulfilling life you have to find balance within these six categories. However, life is a journey, so the goal is not to hit or maintain perfect balance always. This would be unachievable moment to moment. But it is something to consciously work towards. Keep balance in your sights.

The ultimate goal is to find activities that excite and energize you in each of the categories and spend some time on each. Helping my clients in this area also happens to be one of my passions so I could write on and on. But that would go beyond the scope of this book. So, I'll just give a summary of the major categories.

The Physical Dimension of wellness deals with all issues pertaining to your physical body. These include daily exercise (cardiovascular, strength, and flexibility), diet, and medical care. They also include the use and abuse of tobacco, drugs, caffeine and alcohol.

Intellectual Development pertains to involvement in creative, stimulating mental activities. Intellectual stimulation is a form of growth. Continuing to learn for a lifetime is crucial to maintaining intellectual health.

The Social Dimension pertains to contributing to the human community and physical environment. A socially well person has developed healthy ways to interact, react, and live with the people in his or her life. Living well with others might involve, for example, having good boundaries and using assertive communication. (Saying no to set healthy boundaries is a key indicator of success in this dimension!)

Spiritual Development is the quest for meaning and purpose in life. A spiritually well person develops, evolves, and practices his or her religious, political, environmental, and personal beliefs and lives life on purpose.

Emotional Development pertains to awareness and acceptance of your feelings. As an emotionally well person, you maintain quality relationships with others and feel positive about your own life. You also work to decrease levels of stress.

Vocational Development pertains to growth and happiness in your work. A vocationally well person seeks jobs that give personal satisfaction and enrichment.

Catapult Task: How Balanced is Your Life?

How balanced is your life right now? Start by drawing a circle below and then create a pie chart including a section for each of the six dimensions of wellness. Divide the slices based on the amount of time you currently spend in each area. Be truthful!

Which slice is the smallest? Generally, the area with smallest focus has the biggest issues.

It is difficult to do, but try to place a percentage on each of the six dimensions of wellness based on how you would like things to be. The total should equal 100%. Thinking about your interests in this introspective way will help you gain valuable self-knowledge. If you are able to convert your priorities into life changes through conscious choice, you will live a happier more energetic life.

Now, create a list of the activities from each category that seem to give you energy and those that seem to take it away.

Physical:

Intellectual:

Social:

Spiritual:

Emotional:

Vocational:

Of course, as I have already stated, there is no final destination on the path to life balance. It is a journey where you are either moving towards more balance or away. There are times when one area of your life will need additional focus. If you are in a season like this, you must incorporate that into your timelines. Be realistic. If you have a four month old at home and your wife just went back to school to work on her master's degree, this MAY impact your ability to focus as much on your work goals for a period of time. And it will impact your ability whether you acknowledge it or not. So, factor it in to avoid the frustration.

❀

<u>Catapult Task:</u> Designing a Life

If you haven't already done it, take a minute to think about the kind of life you envision for your future. Where are you living? What work are you doing? How much time are you spending on work and how much on other pursuits?

What changes do you need to make over time to help your vision become a reality?

Are there one or two areas in your life that require some additional focus now?

What do you need to do to move towards better balance there?

How much time will it require?

Do you have some special circumstances in one or more areas of your life that will require a bit of extra time and focus?

What do you need to do and how much time will you need to devote?

How long will this situation exist? Is it short term or will it require a year or more of extra accommodation?

Write down some commitments you will make to achieving more life balance:

❦

Assess Your Infrastructures

Another variable that will impact your timelines is the state of your infrastructures. This is the term I use to encompass many aspects that support you in completing your mission. I am referring to the systems and processes that you either have in place or don't. Your infrastructure includes:

- Your communication process with your staff
- Patient flow processes
- Your marketing plan
- Human Resource policies and procedures
- Equipment
- Medical Records (electronic or paper)
- Patient education & communication
- Patient Loyalty Program

Good infrastructures will help you move more quickly toward your mission while non-existent or ineffective infrastructures will slow your progress. In this section, we will evaluate your current infrastructures to determine which ones hinder your progress, support it, or are neutral. From here, you may choose to improve existing infrastructures or implement new ones. Or, you may choose to leave some things as they are. Just know that these infrastructures impact your ability to reach your goals for the better or for the worse. So you must adapt your timelines accordingly. This is another one of those opportunities to get real.

Catapult Task: Assessing Your Infrastructures

Take some time now to evaluate your clinic's infrastructures. Using the list below as a starting point, assess where you are with each aspect of your clinic. Think of as many additional processes as you can beyond what is on the list.

For each category, write the appropriate symbol down from the key. You can write the symbol more than once to indicate an especially good or bad process.

Hinders Progress: - (minus sign)
Supports Progress: + (plus sign)
Neutral: = (equal sign)

Patient Processes

> Scheduling
> Appointment Reminders
> Bring back in to office
> Patient Flow
> Patient Wait Times
> Patient Education
> Patient Loyalty
> Lab result follow up

Billing

Effectively billing all that can be billed

Relationships with insurance companies

Collections process

Medical Records

Timely filing

HIPPA compliant

Forms in order and up to date

Easily accessible and legible

Marketing Initiatives

Patient Events

Referral Program

Advertising

Cross-referral relationships

Mailings

Event sponsorship or participation

Your Team

Drama Free or Drama Full

Focus on mission or focus on staff

Open to change or Avoids change

Discipline Process

Hiring Process
HR Policy Manual
Communication Stream
Accountability Structures
Team organization

Accounting

Maximizing deductions
Orderly files
Tax preparation
Quarterly Taxes
Payroll processing
Minimize financial risk
Cash flow analysis
Profit and loss analysis

Referral Partners

Relationships with: labs, CT, Other Docs, MRI, etc.
Process for receiving results
Communicating results
Follow up
Gratitude Process

◦◦◦

Trusted Advisors

Your gift is serving your patients. Others have very different gifts in areas that can serve you in your practice. Wherever possible, allow these trusted advisors to handle or provide advice for the areas in your clinic that fall outside of your skill set. As an example, once, while doing a presentation, I had a participant raise his hand to share his story. While working in his clinic with a waiting room full of patients the IRS showed up unannounced. He was forced to cancel appointments to deal with the mess he had made doing his own taxes. Note: if this happens to you this is a key indication that it is time to get a good accountant!!

Maintaining good relationships with some key trusted advisors can positively impact your timelines. You can handle everything, but you will not be as effective in those "other areas" as someone who is passionate about the field. And, time spent on anything outside of your passion is time away from what you were born to do.

Here are some key areas where you may want to consider finding trusted advisors if you don't already have them. These advisors can be members of your own staff, consultants that you keep on retainer or specialists who you call on as needed.

> Accountant
> Human Resource Professional
> Process Coach
> Leadership Coach
> Billing Specialist
> Collections Specialist
> Marketing Professional

Attorney

Insurance Professional

Retained Search Professional

Catapult Task: Committing to Action Around Infrastructures

I commit to creating realistic timelines based on my current infrastructures or vow to improve or implement infrastructures that will hasten my progress towards mission.

I choose to put immediate attention towards these infrastructures and will take the following action:

I choose to leave these infrastructures as they are even though they are negative and slow my progress:

These infrastructures will slow my progress in this way:

I will take further action at a later date with these infrastructures:

✌️⌘✍️

Establish Annual and Quarterly Goals

Goals are dreams with deadlines. ~Diana Scharf Hunt

Now that you have done the work and have a clear understanding about how your current infrastructures impact your ability to get work done and have determined which you have identified as areas to focus on now, it is time to create some specific annual goals. From there, you will determine what can be done in the next three months. Each quarter you should create goals that move you powerfully towards your annual goals.

Keep in mind that you are not a lone ranger. Your team members will be assisting you as well. Later in this book, we will be working on delegation strategies. You will also be helping your individual team members set goals. Some of their goals should help you meet yours. In other words, factor in having support in meeting the goals that you set here.

As stated previously, make sure to factor in your life vision and life balance goals into your work. You want your goals to stretch your abilities and maintain your focus but also be realistic.

I know you have heard of the term SMART goals. But, the concept is so important that it deserves a refresher.

Specific: Be clear about what it is you want to accomplish over the course of the next year and quarter. Use precise language and get it written down. Later in the process you will be communicating these goals to your team so that they can participate. You want them to easily identify the outcomes you are working to achieve and how they can assist.

Measurable: If you cannot measure it, there is no clear way to determine whether or not you have achieved it or how far you have left to go. Measurable goals allow you to create milestones and opportunities to celebrate along the journey. This is the motivation you need to make big things happen.

Attainable: The goal can be achieved within the constraints of time, resources, infrastructures, and assistance from your team. I am all about pushing yourself out of your comfort zone and working to excel past what you once thought was not possible. However, there are some limits to what we can accomplish. Goals set either too high or too low become meaningless.

Relevant: Your goals are meaningless unless they are attached to helping you meet your mission and vision. That is the whole point. The interim goals are set to help you create milestones on the way to your bigger mission. Do not include any goals that move you in an opposing direction. Stay on course.

Timely: Specific deadlines must be associated with your goals. This cements pursuit of the achievement and transforms it from a vision or a dream into a concrete action plan. You and your team will rally around deadlines whether they are self-imposed or not.

Additionally, I recommend that you keep it simple. Setting goals does not require flow charts and graphs or pages of documentation. A short list of the specific things you will achieve in the next year, broken down into quarters will suffice. I recommend sticking to around five major SMART goals per year.

If you want to get on a schedule that has you creating your goals along the calendar year or in concert with your fiscal year, that is fine. Just modify the goals for this year to be reasonable for the time remaining in the year. Then start fresh at the next new year with all new annual goals. Repeat the process every year and you will be amazed at your progress!

Catapult Task: **Annual and Quarterly Goals**

My Goals for the next 12 months, attached to Mission and Vision are:

I commit to doing the following in the next quarter in pursuit of my annual goals:

⚮

Protect Your Energy

Most people never run far enough on their first wind to find out they've got a second. Give your dreams all you've got and you'll be amazed at the energy that comes out of you.
– William James

As a good steward of your gifts, you must make a commitment to keep your energy up. You have important work to do. This work requires energy. You cannot create more time but you can create more energy. And once you have optimized your energy, you can focus it to create your desired outcomes.

Can you think back to a time when you felt hopeless? That feeling that you are just sick and tired of the same old thing when it feels like nothing will ever change. What did that feel like energy-wise?

Now think about how much energy you have when it feels like everything is going your way, when you are joyful and almost feel like skipping, when a smile is plastered on your face and you want to laugh at everything around you. You have much more energy when your mood is up.

There is a hierarchy of emotions. In the book *Power V Force* by Dr. David R. Hawkins, M.D., Ph.D., they share the findings of a study done on the vibrational energy created by different emotions. They were actually able to substantiate that emotions like anger, disappointment, revenge, jealousy, and fear all have lower vibrations than the higher-level emotions like love, joy, enthusiasm and hopefulness.

They also conducted some studies where they were able to measure the impact one person with high energy could have on others.

Conversely, the low energy of one individual can impact the energy of others. I'm sure you've experienced this one yourself. You walk into a room where someone is so down and out, they seem to be sucking up any available energy from around them. If you aren't careful, before you know it, you are yawning and feeling low energy too. As a matter of fact, if you do a Google search on protecting your energy, you will find many entries on "energy vampires", a whole new term for the concept!

It sometimes takes an intentional focus to maintain your energy and your patients deserve an energized you. Many are coming to you feeling unwell; they need a boost from you not a bust! You need to protect your energy and focus on maintaining it, both for your patients and for your mission.

Here are some strategies to help maintain your energy.

Intentional Awareness

You have the ability to maintain a high energy level. It is not necessarily something that will happen spontaneously though. Did you know that the average person has approximately 70,000 thoughts per day? Are you even aware that you are empowered to choose the kind of thoughts that you will have? Regardless of circumstance, you can choose your thoughts. That means that you have 70,000 chances to choose thoughts that inspire you or thoughts that bring you down. Thoughts impact your mood and mood helps maintain energy.

Here are two of my favorite phrases:

> "You can't always choose your circumstance but you do get to choose your reaction to your circumstance."

> "Anger is not a required response. It is one that you may or may not choose."

Really take a minute to think about this if it is a new concept for you. There are times that it takes weeks for some of my clients to get this one. They are not convinced until they experience the power for themselves. Sometimes they get angry with me as I try to explain that they cannot control their circumstance but they do get to control their reaction to it. They tell me story after story of frustration. I still come back with, "You can't always choose your circumstance but you do get to choose your reaction." Or, I will say, "Anger is not a required response in that situation. It is what you chose."

Are you thinking this is one of the most ridiculous things you've ever heard? Or maybe you are getting angrier and angrier with me the more you read. Are you thinking about your specific circumstances feeling like, "If she just knew then she would see?" If these are the thoughts you are experiencing then we need to walk you through some smaller steps to get you where you need to be. You need to bust through some walls. Trust me, it is empowering once you get this one.

Once you understand this concept there is no going back. Once you take the blinders off and have this awareness, you are empowered for life. It's a cool one to get! So worth the extra time!

Catapult Task: Taking the Blinders Off (if you need it)

Think of a situation that you experience that routinely causes you frustration. We'll start with a relatively easy one. Some examples might be a know-it-all neighbor, your spouse saying that same thing again and again, a person at the gym who always hogs the machine, traffic tie-ups on your way to work, an employee who complains about the same thing every day, a mother-in-law.

Picture it. Get the frustrations really going. Feel it. Now, stop and think of all of the other emotions that you could CHOOSE to have about this situation. Take a minute to experience each one:

What if this scenario made you paranoid?

What if it made you sad?

What if it made you calm?

What if it made you laugh? Maybe it's the most hilarious thing you've ever heard!

What other emotions might you feel about it?

What other story might you tell yourself about it?

You have all of these emotions, each of these stories, available to you as an option every time you have this experience.

To walk through and fully get each of these steps may take time, maybe even several weeks. I ask you to commit to working on it

- At a minimum, I request that you begin to consider the possibility that you do have options and you are *choosing* your response. – *Can you do at least this?*

- Once you are able to realize it, do the task again and begin to **know**, take in as fact, that you are choosing your response.

- When you are ready, practice choosing a different response. You don't have to commit to it. Just try it on for size. What does it feel like to find traffic a gift? What does it feel like to know that your mother-in-law's comment is the most hilarious thing you've ever heard?

CAUTION – there is no going back from this next step!!

Once you get this concept, you are aware for life!
You are fully empowered.

More joy is available on the other side ~
if you choose it! Are you ready?

- Move forward with full awareness that you are empowered to choose and control your response. You will no longer be able to throw a fit, yell at your team, or throw things without knowing that you are choosing it. Never again, lay on your bed crying without the thought, "I will choose to feel this way for now."

⸎⸎

Moving Forward

Now that you know that you have the power to choose your response, choose to think and be in a way that allows you to focus on success. Pay attention to your own energy. You get to tell the story of your life. Why not choose thoughts that keep your energy up?

Be aware of the energy of others and put a barrier between you and those with low energy. Do not allow those with low energy to pull yours down.

Back to the experience of walking into a room that has been hijacked by low energy people, you can feel your own energy begin to drain if you let it. Without intentional focus on your own energy, you will lose it and have to rejuvenate. Instead of allowing others to suck you down where they are, put a boundary around your high energy and provide them with the opportunity to increase their energy.

Intentional Choice - How to choose

You now know that you get to choose. If your energy dips and you are having, "one of those days," know that it is your choice to stay there or not. Let's talk about some strategies to help you choose differently. Regardless of your circumstances, you have the opportunity to choose with intention.

Throughout your day, you continually process your circumstances and the things you tell yourself about those circumstances make up the story of your life. The story you tell yourself in each situation will help to create your response. Your response creates your emotion. Your emotional state is a factor that determines your level of energy.

Circumstance = Chosen Thoughts (Story) = Response = Emotion = Energy Level

The stuff that we experience doesn't have meaning until we assign the meaning. Assigning the meaning is what I call telling the story. It's the story that makes a happening emotional. That story will either create positive, empowering emotions or negative, victimizing emotions.

We also create a story in our mind to make sense out of events that we witness. We work from assumption. I love to work with my clients on this one. People spend much of their lives in the world of assumption without even realizing it. Until they work with me, that is! Someone makes a face in a meeting and we assume that it means one thing; we then begin to relate to that person as if our assumption is fact. We have now altered the relationship based on our assumption.

We all have filters through which we tend to see the world. Now that you are aware of the fact that you choose your story, you can begin to look around your filters. You will also begin to see how your filters will create patterns in the stories that you tell yourself.

Let's start with an example outside of ourselves. It is often easier.

Example

You are stuck in traffic. A driver speeds up the shoulder of the expressway with his headlights flashing. His face is tight. What story do you tell?

Some people have a victim mentality. If the above scenario occurs, they may have a tendency to tell a story that the world is against them. That person just wanted to get past them.

If you have a filter that everyone is a jerk you might think that the person is self-centered and is whizzing down the side of the road because they think they are the only ones who have to be anywhere important.

If, on the other hand, you have a compassion filter, you may decide that the person is rushing to the hospital and the face they are making is the result of worry.

A very competitive person may decide that the person is acting like Mario Andretti and will take up chase!

Spend some time figuring out what your filters are and where you are living in the world of assumption. Make the commitment to stay out of the world of assumption and do some fact-finding whenever possible.

Sympathetic vs. Empathetic – Compassion Fatigue

You may be involved with emotionally demanding situations on a daily basis. Be intentional about how you respond. You can be empathetic with your patients and staff but to maintain your own level of energy you must not be sympathetic.

Zig Ziglar uses a great analogy to illustrate the difference between sympathetic and empathetic. Visualize the deck of a cruise ship. You come across a seasick passenger leaning over the railing. A sympathetic person looks at them, feels their pain and must join them at the railing. An empathetic person sees them and feels sorry for them but maintains an emotional distance. This emotional distance allows them to assess the situation and then to be of service to the person. The empathetic person maintains his or her own energy and well-being.

You must do the same. If, all day, you are being dragged down by stories you hear from patients or getting sucked in to drama in your office, you are not your best self. You must keep an emotional distance with appropriate boundaries to create the space to act as a resource. The truth is if you don't manage your energy, your mind will do it for you. To preserve yourself, you will create a protective barrier that no longer allows you to feel for your patients. This is apathy. You do not want to live life from here.

Your profession has even coined a phrase for the phenomenon,

"Compassion Fatigue" where your own spiritual and emotional energy is drained to the point where you can no longer experience joy or feel for others.

So the key is to set boundaries around your energy. Care from an empathetic place and make sure that you are carving out time to rejuvenate yourself and maintain some amount of life balance so that you don't develop compassion fatigue.

Focus On What You Control

Along your journey to your mission, you will come across many obstacles and things you wish were different. Some obstacles will be within your power to change. Other obstacles, however, are simply out of your control.

While it is difficult to focus only on what you control, it makes sense; put your energy and focus where you can have an impact.

Byron Katie has written a fabulous book that, in a nutshell, is all about accepting what is so and then moving on. It is called "Loving What Is" I often use her concepts with my clients. They are simple in nature but difficult to live out. However, perfecting the art will allow you to stay more fully connected to your passion.

When I describe her concept to a client, I hold one hand flat in the air and hit it with my other hand fisted. The flat hand acts like a wall and represents reality or the things that my client can not change. The fisted hand represents the client, frustrated and wishing reality would change. The thinking when we are bumping against reality is often, "They should act different, insurance companies should pay more freely; government should get rid of red tape."

The problem is that reality does not change, whether we feel frustrated by it or we ignore it and move on. If it is out of our control, our energy is wasted when we bump up against it and allow it to frustrate.

You could continue to waste energy and focus on being frustrated and thinking that you could run the world better. But you don't, so, energy and focus placed here is wasted.

This is not to say that you should turn a blind eye to the larger issues of the world. You can certainly be an advocate for change. You can join forces with others to work towards insurance reform. But the time, energy, and focus, that you put there must be intentional. Do what you can and then move on. Hope for the best without attachment to any particular outcome. If you are too attached to a specific outcome, you will be frustrated or disappointed if any other outcome occurs. Do what you can and move on. Conserve your energy and focus for things within your control.

I teach my clients this simple exercise to determine where best to focus energy. You can follow a process daily.

Just apply these few simple questions to any daily activity, follow through based on your answers and you'll experience more focused energy and peace.

Here are the questions. If none of the resulting answers is "move forward" then move on. Here's how it goes:

1. Is any part of this in my control?

   Yes – Move forward

   No – Move on

2. Can I provide support or advocacy?

3. Yes – Move forward without too much attachment to one specific outcome

   No – Move on

4. I am a valuable resource. Is this worthy of my time and energy?

   Yes – Move forward

   No – Move on

5. Am I able to make space for this given my current set of priorities?

   Yes – Move forward

   No – Move on

Catapult Task: What is in my Control?

Let's take a global look at what is in your control and what is not.

This will help you quickly clear your slate. Keep focusing your energy only on those things that you can impact. Generally, we end up with plenty on our plate with those things we can control. Why bother adding extra with the things we can do nothing about?

First, I want you to think about all the things that you cannot control:

- You cannot control the AMA.
- You cannot control the health insurance industry.
- You cannot control what time your next patient arrives.

All of the things that are out of your control are taking up valuable space in your head. You gain focus by eliminating all that clutter that keeps you bouncing around all day long. I want you to focus on all the things in your life and in your day-to-day work that you cannot control and below I want you to write each one of them down. Get out an extra sheet of paper if you need to! (because you just might!)

The Things I Cannot Control:

Take a few minutes to focus on these things and really think about how futile it is to worry about them and to waste your energy on them. They are outside of your control and the sooner you are able to let go of that, the sooner you can start to affect change in your own life and in your own practice. There are many things, on the other hand, that you CAN change. Many things in your life you can affect, improve, and change all together.

- You can change how you respond to conflict in the office
- You can change what time to you get to work each morning
- You can adjust job titles to make sure each member of your team is fully using their talents
- You can communicate clear expectations to your team
- You an communicate and stick to an appointment cancellation policy

The Things I CAN Control:

Take a long, hard look at the list that you have just made. These are the things you should be focused on throughout your day to assure that your energy is being used effectively.

⌒◦◦⌒

Practice the Art of Gratitude

Practicing the art of gratitude is about maintaining a focus on all that you can appreciate. Consider starting a gratitude journal. Write in it first thing in the morning or at night before you go to bed. Or, keep it in your car and jot things down while you are sitting at a light. As you spend your day looking for things to be grateful for, you will find your focus magically shifted. It will become easier and easier to find positive things.

I have had times in my life where I was really struggling to keep my focus positive, when outer circumstances were especially stressful. I have actually kept my gratitude journal right next to me all day, writing in it throughout the day or each time I thought of something else for which to be grateful. And it has worked. Spending even a portion of a day doing that can shift your focus for a few weeks. For real, it is magical! It really is. Try it!

Still having trouble thinking of things? Here are some ideas:

- Beautiful day
- Rain to water the grass for free
- The transportation that got you to your destination
- Family
- Friends
- Hitting your patient volume goals
- Having great patient flow
- Healing a patient
- Your legs that carried you into the building
- Your hands that help heal
- Your staff members
- The food you had for breakfast
- The trees and flowers
- The people who plow snow off the streets
- The teachers in your children's school
- The crossing guard who helps your child stay safe
- The roof over your head
- The bed you slept in last night
- Coffee
- Tea
- Your cell phone
- Internet access
- Your spouse
- Your health

- Your kids
- Heat or air conditioning in your building

Maintain a Focus on Celebration

Putting your focus on celebration will also increase your level of vibrational energy. Remember, you can easily move yourself up the hierarchy of emotional energy by intentionally choosing a higher level mood. Why stay stuck in a low vibration emotion of resentment when you can feel the higher energy of celebration?

And, by celebrate, I don't mean throw a big party with hats, noisemakers and all kinds of food and drinks. You can have a one-person celebration sitting at your desk. Just take one minute to stop and think, "Ahhhhh, I am awesome", or, "We made great headway yesterday." Just feel yourself relax and enjoy the accomplishment, the progress, even if it is just for a moment.

That's it. That's a celebration.

So be the kind of leader who looks for reasons to celebrate with your team. There will always be things to work on, goals not yet achieved. I'm not suggesting you turn a blind eye. But you can't put one hundred percent of your focus there. That just makes for a frustrated leader.

Without intentionally choosing to spend time celebrating, it is so easy to get caught in the grind of just doing without realizing the progress made.

Catapult Task: Celebration and Gratitude

I commit to the following to add celebration to my practice this week:

I am grateful for these things right now:

COCO

Expectations vs. Experience: Life in the Gap

Another potential for energy drain can happen when our expectations do not match our experiences. I call this "life in the gap" and it is where we spend most of our waking hours. We traverse the journey of life creating expectations about everything and everyone around us. Our expectations are how we think things should be, how we assume they will be or how we want them to be.

The problem is that our actual experiences rarely, if ever, match our expectations.

So, you prepare for a vacation and create an expectation that you will spend hours on the beach only to experience terrible weather.

Or, you implement a new billing system and expect it to have an immediate positive impact in your clinic only to find that the learning curve is much longer than anticipated and that your team is resistant to the change.

Much of our experience of life is determined by how we react in the gap. The more we hold fast to our original expectations the more opportunity we have for disappointment, frustration, resentment or outright anger. All of which deplete our energy.

If, on the other hand, we can be a bit looser with our expectations, we are able to find more joy and fulfillment with the unexpected. Often, things out of our control occur that take us into the gap. So, being frustrated with them just uses our energy unnecessarily.

To use a very simple and silly illustration I will talk about my hair. If you looked at the picture on the book cover you may have noticed that I have curly hair. If you know anything about curly hair, you probably know that it has a mind of its own. I really have little control over what it will look like each day. Regardless of what I am up to, how important the client, or the size of the audience I am speaking for, my hair is going to do what my hair is going to do. If I held fast to a specific expectation of my hair looking a certain way for any given occasion I would spend most days very frustrated, upset or even embarrassed. Therefore, I must be loose with my expectations for my own sanity. The look of my hair is largely out of my control.

I told you this would be a silly example. Let's hit closer to home. I am sure you have experienced patients who do not meet your expectations. You feel like you have gone above and beyond for them and still they are not appreciative at all. They may have a sense of entitlement or experience no power in their lives so assert it with you whenever they can. Therefore, to continue to hold tight to an expectation that they will treat you a certain way is just setting yourself up for failure. To save your sanity and your energy, you must release and allow them to have their own life experience. They are going to react how they are going to react regardless of what you think is appropriate. So, you can experience them as they are or you can feel frustration that they are not handling life as you believe they should.

Or, think about your patients who do not follow your professional advice. Perhaps you have had to stand back helpless as their health deteriorates. Your expectation is that they would value their health and follow your recommendations. Nevertheless, your experience is that they do what they want. Their actions are out of your control. Holding tight to that one expectation will just cause frustration and grief.

Therefore, it is in your best interest to preserve your energy by letting go of tightly held expectations that only lead to disappointment.

Later in the book, we will cover the topic of Leading in the Gap where you can and should exert more control. In the meantime, be aware and know that in almost every moment you are in the gap. How will you choose to respond?

Passion from the Platform: Letting Go of Your Energy-Busting Emotions

Often by the time a client hires me they are in total frustration mode. So much has gotten in the way of their mission that they feel hopeless. They feel like they must be on overdrive, fighting and clawing their way to reach their mission.

Some create adversaries where there are none, defining any person who stands as a barrier to success as having evil intent. Upon further review we are able to determine that often these "adversaries" have sound reason to back their stance and with good communication win-win solutions can be achieved.

Many are also discouraged because they do not feel heard. A common next step is to dive deeper into exactly what that looks like. Often, we discover that my client is verbally fighting so hard for their vision that they are not hearing others. When we do not hear others, they often do not hear us. If the only strategy is to continue to speak louder or longer in an attempt to be heard there is no progress only more frustration.

When you are single-mindedly pursuing your mission and experiencing the journey as negatively charged you can enter a negative spiral, a frenzied fight to reach your goals. This is not passion from the platform.

As we work to remove these negative emotions, often, initially my clients want to hold on. They tell me, "But I am a passionate person! I care so much about my patients! I can't let go of that drive!" Over time they have acclimated themselves to feeling driven by anger and frustration and fear that without these emotions they will not be motivated.

It takes work to get them to understand that none of that anger and frustration is passion! These are not necessary emotions to help you meet your mission. They are emotions resulting from the focus on the barriers to achieving mission rather than the joyful journey.

On the contrary, passion is: joy, contentment, focus, engagement, and positive energy.

Emotions are good. They give us information. However, if your entire life is dictated by your emotions, you will be all over the road. Moods and emotions can shift with more than just our circumstance. Sometimes we are just eating the wrong foods or lacking sleep. Being overwhelmed can create new emotions and without healthy boundaries in your relationships, your emotions can swing along with important people in your life.

Constantly reacting to your emotions can change your relationships. Frustration taken out on staff and family members leads to conflict and requires you to go into clean up mode. All of which takes your energy away from working on your mission.

I am here to tell you that moving towards your mission DOES NOT require fighting, clawing, being frustrated or overwhelmed. In fact, you will be moving more powerfully towards mission if you remove that junk and put all of your energy towards your passion, less energy towards the fighting and the clawing and more towards tenacity and perseverance.

This is my definition of Passion from the Platform. I am a very visual person so when I describe the concept it is what I see. I imagine my client standing on a large, sturdy, elevated stage. The elevated stage, or platform, is this sturdy, stable foundation from which to communicate, make decisions. Life on the platform is good! It is a place where you are free from your emotions, where you have good objectivity.

To arrive and live on the platform takes an adjustment to how you react to your emotions, how you view yourself and how you communicate.

I encourage my clients to pay attention to their emotions but to analyze them before getting into action around them. Ask some questions like:

- "Am I bumping up against one of my filters?"
- "Could I tell myself a different story here?"
- "Am I hearing others or just fighting to be heard?"
- "Am I in the gap? What is in my control and what is not?"
- "Am I attempting to create a feeling of passion from frustration because that is my habit?"
- "Is this person really an adversary? What are their true intentions?"

Communication from the platform involves hearing first and then speaking, seeing the conversation as a journey rather than an end all be all. From this place, there is room to find common ground and to consider creative solutions together. Relationships work better. There is room to hear another's point of view, understand it, consider it, and look for ways to incorporate it.

What battles are you waging?

You can wage those battles manically, fired up with anger and frustration or you can wage them sensibly, with tenacity and a focus on your end goal.

Life on the platform is the place to wage your war. Focus stays on your mission and energy stays positive. Relationships endure and grow stronger as your communication transforms. There is room for more creative problem solving as all people are given a voice and are heard.

Catapult Task: Living on the Platform

My emotions are keeping me off the platform:

I commit to reviewing my emotions before acting on them:

I am creating frustration or drama in place of passion:

I am not hearing others or considering their perspectives in these areas:

I commit to these changes in my communication:

I am creating adversaries where there are none here:

I commit to seeking common ground here:

⤳∞⤶

Lead Well

If your actions inspire others to dream more,
learn more, do more and become more, you are a leader.
~John Quincy Adams

Now that you have clarified your mission and developed a game plan for your clinic, it is time to put it all into action. It is one thing to have it all in your head. Now you need to communicate your mission and game plan in a way that inspires your staff to excellence and creates targeted focus of time, energy, and effort from your team.

As a leader, you must exhibit this focus as well, as you accept nothing less than excellence from your team and require them to fire up for your mission. You may get some resistance, it might even look similar to the baby in the car seat example you read earlier, but, at the end of the day, a tenacious leader will not take a side step around an employee.

This, my friend, is leadership. Without a great leadership style, you are limited. There is only so much that one person can do.

What does it take to be a great leader? There are thousands of books on the topic. In this chapter, we will boil it all down to the basics. Great leadership requires making sound decisions and sticking to them. Going forward your decisions will be based on moving your clinic towards a specific target. There still may be some missteps but most of the time you will be right in the ballpark rather than all over the road. The next step is to lead your team effectively so that your capacity to do your work increases exponentially.

Lead Well with a Heart to Heal and Serve

First things first. We need to work on your mindset. You have the right and the duty to lead in your clinic. You must take back your power. Because, if you are like the hundreds of other health professionals

I have worked with or spoken to, you are frustrated about life in your workplace but feeling like there is nothing you can do about it. At every turn, you are telling yourself a story about why it can't be fixed. We need to change that now. None of the work you've done can create change unless you get this concept.

This is one area where your heart to serve REALLY gets in the way. Often, the leaders I work with feel like they cannot get staff to do what they need them to do. They hide, end up doing everything themselves to make sure it's done right, and feel resentful and over-whelmed. Eventually they explode and take their frustration out on their staff. But, without consistent follow through or consequences, the explosion creates no change. The team just waits for the episode to be over and goes on, business as usual. It becomes nothing more than a cycle.

Sometimes there is no explosion. The health care leader will hold all of the resentment in and feel worse and worse. Health issues crop up; they become distant in their clinic and at home. The frustration, and resentment build and build and they become disempowered.

It does not have to be this way!

This is your business. It is your clinic, your vision, your mission, your life. Your staff members are an extension of you. They help create the perception that your patients have of you and your clinic. Are they doing a good job or not? If you are tolerating less than what you deserve – why? Stop!! Now!!!

This is a time to bust through your fear. To move your mission for-ward you must be ready to go to the mat for your clinic. Ideally, as you begin to truly lead and align your staff with your mission, they will rise to the occasion. They will feel inspired and realize it is a privilege to work for you, and that to continue to do so they must follow the new rules and conform to the new culture. But, they might not. They may continue in their current patterns, focusing on themselves and the interpersonal dramas they create.

Will your team change or will they continue with their current behaviors, this is the big "what if?" It is often the fear of this "what if?" that stops my health care leader clients.

Does this sound familiar? "If I lead differently, they might not follow. What if they don't follow? I might need to fire them and I can't do that. So, I will just keep things as they are. We are getting by. Things are fine the way they are."

I am telling you, it is not fine! And, the problem is, this fear is making you give away your power to your team. If you are not willing to go to the mat, if you are not willing to do what it takes to create the clinic you desire and the life you envisioned, you are the one doing all of the bobbing and the weaving to your staff's whim. They are in charge of your workplace culture and they are setting the direction for your clinic. Where is their focus now? Is it on your patients or on themselves? Is time and energy spent on interpersonal drama between team members rather than on healing your patients? Is this what you want?

The truth about fear is that avoidance does not make it go away. It just makes it bigger.

I watched this in action with my oldest son. When he was about five years old, he became very afraid of thunderstorms. It got quite bad. He would actually sweat and shake and would hide in our basement.

Over time, he became more and more afraid. His "what if?" must have been huge! He continued to react to the fear and it got even bigger. He became afraid when it rained, because, if it rained it might thunder. He began hiding in the basement anytime it rained.

Eventually, he became afraid when it was cloudy. If it's cloudy, it might rain. If it rains, it might thunder. He would leave our pool to go inside and hide in the basement. After a while, he became afraid if it was windy. Wind might bring clouds, clouds might bring rain and rain might bring thunder. He would leave the beautiful sunny day and leave his friends to hide in the basement.

I am happy to report that he has busted this one. But it took walking backwards through the levels of fear that he had developed. He learned that it was okay to be in wind, it might NOT bring clouds. Then it was okay to be under clouds. They might NOT bring rain. And so on.

Do you see how the fear is like a blob? It becomes bigger and more consuming the more we accommodate it.

- What fears are lingering in your practice and in your life?
- Where is your accommodation of your fear altering the course of your work?

Look back and see the journey that has taken you out of the driver's seat in your clinic. Have you just moved to the passenger seat or are you all the way in the trunk? It's a slippery slope accommodating your fears.

Here are some of the common fears I run across with my clients when dealing with staff issues. It's what ultimately brings them to me. Any sound familiar?

- They might get angry or defensive if I ask them to change.
- They might not like me.
- They might have a nervous breakdown.
- They might not listen.
- They'll just keep doing it the same way anyway.
- They are going through a hard time; they might feel worse.
- I can't fire so and so, they are the niece to my long time patient of 10 years.
- They know everything about my clinic.
- I'll have to hire someone new, it will take forever, and they'll be just as bad or worse.
- I'll have to teach someone new. It takes too long.
- They might go work for a competitor and take all of my patients with them.

I am going to hypothesize that you have fear stopping you in this area. I know that you do not know all of the steps to fix your staff issues yet. It's okay. You will. As you progress, this book will continue to build your knowledge and skills. However, for this chapter I am asking you to explore your fears, bust through them and move forward. Can you commit to doing that?

You have the power, *all the power*, in your clinic.

- Will it be easy? Maybe not, but few things worthy of achieving are.
- Will there be a time of transition? Yes.
- Will there be some negative fall out? Possibly.
- Will the fallout be worse than what you are experiencing day

to day now? No!
- Will it be better in the long run? Yes!

Without exception, every client I have worked with who has followed the steps you are about to take has been happier and more successful as a result. And all have found it easier than they imagined. Because, as is often the case, our fearful version of what might be is far worse than the reality of what is.

Are you ready to take back the power in your clinic, hold your staff accountable and lead?

Catapult Task: Evaluating My Fears

The problem with fear is that often we focus all of our energy on avoiding it and no time at all on determining exactly what it is we are afraid of or how real the threat.

My fear about truly leading my staff and holding them accountable is (*be specific*):

Reality Check. What is the worst-case scenario? What are the chances of this happening – *REALLY*?!

Would it really matter that much if this did happen?

I suffer these consequences by allowing this fear to win:

My clinic & mission suffer these consequences by allowing this fear to win:

I commit to taking these steps to diminish this fear and expand my influence. Start big or small, just get moving to expand your life!

What successes have you experienced? Keep track of these until you get good at busting through your fears. They will give you fuel to keep playing larger and larger.

✂

Lead Well Through the "Life is Hard" Sympathy Card

There is no use whatever trying to help people who do not help themselves. You cannot push anyone up a ladder unless he be willing to climb himself. ~ Andrew Carnegie

Another barrier I find to great leadership among healthcare professionals is what I will call the "Life is Hard" sympathy card. Healthcare leaders, in particular, fall prey to this one easily and allow their staff to play the hand too often. That heart to heal and serve makes you want to save the world and help your employees at every turn. You are wracked with guilt if you do not do all that you can for someone. Unfortunately, often what I've seen is that it goes too far. You do not want to be an enabler. And, in particular, you don't want to put your clinic, patients and business at risk to accommodate employees who are playing the "Life is Hard" sympathy card.

They wreak havoc in your clinic by coming to work crying and whining about the latest crisis in their lives. They pull all of the focus onto themselves. You'd love to have these staff members and the rest of your team focus some of their energy on your sick and hurting patients but you feel so bad for them. Maybe this time they'll get it together. You allow them to be unproductive, give them extra time off, and ignore their tardiness. Maybe you listen to their problems too but at a minimum allow other team members time away from work to lend an ear. I even had one client give a "Life is Hard" sympathy card employee a big bonus every year to try to help. She was a single mom struggling through one self-inflicted crisis after another. The result of that one was no change in behavior, no appreciation, no productivity, just a sense of entitlement and anger when the bonuses stopped.

The problem is that, more often than not, it's the employee's choices that are putting them in these bad situations and work is not the place to go for sympathy and support. Yes, of course we can care about one another. This isn't about being a cold fish and turning off your heart. However, at work the focus needs to be on patients. If these employees have no time or energy left for your patients, they need to go to a place where it is appropriate to talk about their issues, where they can get the support they need to change. They don't need a shoulder to cry on as they repeat the same patterns over and over.

Many times the employees using the "Life is Hard" sympathy card are allowed to behave with complete disregard to those around them because your servant's heart makes you feel guilt if you cannot help. You can't discipline or terminate them because you feel bad for them; they need the job.

Here are just some of the reasons I've heard for not holding someone accountable - repeatedly, I might add:

- She's a single mom. She really needs this job.
- Her husband is an alcoholic.
- He's filing for bankruptcy.
- She's been having issues with an abusive boyfriend.
- Her kids have been getting into trouble at school.
- Her kids keep calling her because they need her.
- They are in foreclosure.

- His wages are being garnished.
- Her family won't have anything to do with her.
- He has nowhere else to turn.
- She's really upset because her boyfriend is cheating on her.

Is all of this tough stuff? Yep. Do you think it's possible that some of your rock star employees have gone through some of this as well but chose to be professional and put their problems aside while at work? It isn't a requirement to share your personal dramas at work. But, it's serving some of your employees well if you continue to accommodate them as a result.

Those using the "Life is Hard" sympathy card need to want the job as bad as you want them to have the job. If they really need it, they need to make the right choices to keep it. You can't keep accommodating them for their choices by working to make the job convenient for them because you fear the thought of them being without the income.

They don't get to set the bar for behavior, energy, and productivity in your clinic; you do. What level of performance do they need to maintain to keep the job that they need so terribly? Where does their focus need to be? If they really want the job, they will rise to the occasion and do what they need to do to keep it.

If they don't make the right choice there should be no guilt. They are given a choice. Here's the standard of work required; now choose. Your team members have the free will to choose to do what they need to do to keep the job or not. It is your job to clearly communicate these requirements.

If your fear makes you waiver and change your expectations of a staff member you are allowing another person to dictate the culture and direction of your clinic. Their choices have put their life in shambles. Do you really want them dictating *anything* that happens in your workplace? Is this really what you want?

I was recently working with a clinic where a long-term employee was about to be terminated and the manager was wracked with guilt. The employee was an X-ray tech and had let her certification lapse. This was obviously a huge liability issue for the clinic. The manager had given her 2 *years* (yes, you are reading that right, years) to do what she needed to do to renew the certification and had offered to pay for the classes.

The employee chose to do nothing, took not one class. Instead, she chose to spend her time and energy walking around telling everyone how her employer was trying to push her out of her job.

- Was every effort made to help this employee? Yes.
- Did the employee have final control over taking the classes or not? Yes.
- Who is at fault for the termination? The employee.
- Is it reasonable for a clinic to take on the liability of utilizing an uncertified x-ray tech to accommodate this staff member's desire to continue with status quo? No!
- Is it acceptable for her to rile up the other staff members with her denial? No!
- Should the manager feel guilty? No!

Do not take on guilt where you have no control.

You cannot control other people's actions and you cannot control their perceptions. They will have their own life experience and you need to allow that. Sometimes their perceptions will cause them to be angry with you. You have to be okay with that. Sometimes those perceptions are the defense mechanism that keeps them stuck where they are. They are using the flawed perception to feel like a victim. A victim is unable to take action or make change. They don't want to take ownership of their own lives so they need to place blame on someone else. At times, that someone might be you. Let them, but do not take it on as guilt!

Now, being okay with their anger is not the same as being okay with them acting out because of that anger. Being okay with their anger is about not letting fear of their anger stop you from holding them to reasonable standards regardless of their circumstance. You are absolutely allowed and encouraged to stop them from acting out as a result of their anger. It's about setting boundaries and sticking to them. An employee who is angry about being held accountable to a work standard can be angry but they cannot act out because of that anger. They need to act professionally and appropriately. Do not tolerate storming, stomping, throwing, slamming, eye rolling, yelling, swearing or anything resembling these actions. There are more consequences if a staff member cannot act professionally. Period. (We will be talking about these consequences in subsequent chapters).

You set the standard for this too. They can then choose to act appropriately or not. If they have a lot of bad stuff going on in their lives and really need the job, then they'd better make the right choice. They may not. It's their choice. No guilt.

Got it?

Catapult Task: Analyzing the Impact of My Accommo-dations

Let's get clear on the full impact your accommodations are having on your clinic, team and patients. I bet you haven't taken the time to sit down and pull it all together. Are you ready? It may be much bigger than you think. It's a necessary exercise though. Seeing the full impact in one spot will help create the motivation that you need to change. You know what they say, "The pain of staying the same has to be worse than the pain of the change."

Let's create enough pain to motivate you through the fear of some team members being unhappy, angry, upset, sad, or throwing temper tantrums.

I am making these accommodations as a result of the "Life is Hard" sympathy card:

These accommodations are having this impact on my clinic:

These accommodations are having this impact on my team:

These accommodations are having this impact on my rock star employees:

These accommodations are having this impact on my patients:

These accommodations are having this impact on the employee I am making them for:

I will maintain appropriate standards and allow my team to choose freely. I commit to making these changes without guilt:

〜◆〜

Lead Well with Decisiveness

Allow others to have input in your decisions, but at the end of the day they are yours to make and own. At some point the conversation stops. Once the decision is made, the team follows. No more discussion.

This one can be a bit difficult and there will be transition if you've been a leader who allows staff to have the ultimate decision whether on purpose or by default. They may act out at first but keep at it and keep communicating that your decisions are final.

I recently had a client work through this transition. He had been leading by consensus. But the culture had grown to require too much discussion and not enough action. If not everyone could agree, nothing got done. Slowly, he took back his power. He would allow some discussion but would then make the final decision when it was required and expected the staff to move forward.

The problem was that based on experience, they still thought it was debate time. Sometimes they overturned his decision and acted based on their own. We realized together that he needed to make one more announcement about expectations. At times, he would allow the staff to make the final decision. On certain things, however, his decisions were going to be the final say. Period. No more discussion. No more debate. Just get into action. He enlisted his office manager in the new strategy as well. Staff would routinely come to her and say, "You know, I think…" and she would say, "I'll talk to the doctor about it." That just perpetuated the culture of debate. They came up with a key phrase that meant discussion over and he got his office manager on board to say, "Well, that is the final decision. We need to get into action."

If this sounds familiar, you may need to follow a similar strategy to take back the reigns.

Lead Well with Integrity

Integrity is about saying what you will do and doing what you say. Another key ingredient is, owning it when you do not follow this simple rule.

Often my clients intend to lead with integrity but things get in the way. The good news for you is that we have already covered and done some skill building around the main barriers to living and working with good integrity.

If you have a clear mission and vision, it is much easier to be decisive and hold fast to commitments you make. Decisions made based on your mission and vision should be easy to keep. You will have the tenacity to follow through. The waffling comes when you lack clear mission and vision. There are more missteps, more opportunities to change course. This should happen less so you will be much more apt to say one thing and then do it.

The tenacity that comes with following your passion and a clear mission/vision will also help you walk your talk. Hurdles, barriers, and challenges will no longer require you to change direction altogether. Over time, your team will learn to trust your words more and more.

Fighting the fear and following through with your team will help you live with integrity as well. Commitments to change direction have probably been squelched because of your inability to hold staff accountable. Over time, as they see you mean business, they will learn to take your word as law. You will now be much more likely to say something and stick to it with your staff.

And, if you find you have miscommunicated or made a mistake – communication – communication – communication. Own it and move on. No big deal. Sweeping things under the rug can help in the moment but does nothing to build trust or help you lead with integrity over the long haul.

Lead Well With Respect

I encourage my clients to work from the assumption that their employees do want to do a good job. I believe that most do. Sometimes, however, things are standing in their way; Processes that are not working, indecisive leaders (that's you), and expectations set too low.

I have been in many clinics where the group norm is to whine, complain and place blame on others. Usually there is at least one employee who fits right in to this environment and probably needs to go but often it is the group norm that has sucked people in and caused them to behave in ways that they normally wouldn't. Recalibrating the culture often does wonders immediately.

Or, your rock stars are frustrated, overwhelmed and just don't care any longer.

So, create the environment that supports your team working to their potential and treat them with the respect they deserve.

If you have become frustrated and are acting out by yelling, screaming, throwing temper tantrums or, worse, verbally abusing your staff, this is not leadership! And it is NOT lending itself to a warm, nurturing environment for your patients.

Stop!

As the leader, you are the role model for how team members will treat each other. Showing respect requires good tone of voice, volume, body language and words.

Trust your team to do a good job and make sure they have the tools to do it. We will be covering this more in later chapters, so don't worry about all of this now. Just know that leading with respect is the bar that I'm setting for you regardless of circumstance. The consequence of poor behavior is a professional response in which you reiterate expectations and ask them to either correct their behavior or follow a discipline process. Throwing a temper tantrum at your team is not an appropriate response.

Even the employees who are on their way out deserve respect. There's no need for yelling. It's just not a good fit for them. Walk them calmly through the discipline process as you firmly stick to your expectations and then release them to work elsewhere. Let them leave with their dignity.

Lead Well with Precise Language

Your team cannot read your mind. Be clear and precise with your language so they know where the organization is heading and what you need from them to get there. I once worked with a leader who made it a game of seeing whether his executive team could figure out what he already had in mind for next steps. He somehow got an ego boost from it. He even laughed at them when they got it wrong. On a personal level, he seemed to gain from it, somehow. From a business perspective, not smart. He was allowing his team to make missteps, waste time and energy all to get a chuckle. His focus was in the wrong place.

The goal is actually to communicate well so that your team can execute well. A quick side comment grumbled as you pass in the hall is not optimal communication. And feeding them crumbs to see whether they can figure the rest out or testing their mind reading skills is not the best for your business.

If you are suffering from a lack of confidence in your leadership or are falling victim to the "life is hard" sympathy card, you may find yourself using what I call tentative language. You are uncomfortable holding your staff accountable and making requests. Maybe you think they are already too busy.

Tentative language is using words that water down your message. It takes away the punch that they could have and leaves staff feeling unclear.

Examples of words and phrases that create tentative language:

- Sort of
- If you get a chance
- Kind of
- If you can
- Maybe

Your intent may be to soften the request but the message you end up delivering is that your task is not really that important. "When you get the chance" may feel friendly in the moment but your team is hearing that they have leeway. They may never get the chance so that task may go unfinished forever. Is that really what you want? If not, communicate the expectation more precisely.

I have had so many clients express frustration with their team's ability to follow through only to find that the culprit is the language the leader is using. A small tweak and they are frustration-free.

Lead Well in the Gap

We have covered the topic of *living* in the gap, when your experiences do not match your expectations. Now it is time to talk about *leading* in the gap. There is a difference because you often have more power as a leader in the gap if you choose to exercise it.

First, let's take a look at some of the things that take you into the gap as a leader.

Perhaps you expect your team to complete tasks to a specific quality standard but they do not. Or, you set goals and they do not meet them. Perhaps you assume that they will behave professionally because it is work but you find that they often treat your workplace like a playground. Or, you expect them to accept a new process or system but then find that they are resistant to any change.

What are your tendencies today when you experience the gap as a leader? Do you:

- Get into action?

- Hide?
- Feel like a victim and say, "What can I do?"
- Go into denial and tell yourself that it is not really that bad?
- Complain to people other than the offenders? Otherwise known as venting.
- Feel resentful?
- Look at yourself first?

Your response is important because often, you, as leader, have the power to increase the gap or decrease it based on your response. You have many options from which to choose. Let's look at some to determine why there may be a gap and then we'll explore the best actions to take to bring your expectations and experiences closer together.

First let's look at some things that can create or increase the gap:

- **Unrealistic Expectations:** We have already looked at some of your tendencies as a leader. Did you confess to being a perfectionist? If so, you often have expectations set too high. You will spend a lot of time in the gap as your team struggles to meet your unrealistic goals.
- **Expectations Were Not Communicated:** Do you use good delegation strategies? Does your team know the target or are they shooting in the dark and failing to meet your hidden agenda? We will be covering this topic later.
- **No Call to Action:** If you give no clear call to action the "get around to it" time frame may never happen for your team. Are you using tentative language that minimizes your action message? Your communication could be creating your gap.
- **Group Norms:** Does your team have some beliefs that create

a gap? Perhaps they believe nothing is ever good enough anyway so why even try? Or, if you have a very negative culture they could be engaging in some sabotage or work slow down activities to preserve a job with you without having to work hard. I have seen it happen many times! A new employee starts and is told, "Don't work that quickly. They'll expect it all the time."

- **Knowledge, Skills and Abilities:** Maybe your team is lacking the key knowledge, skills and abilities to do a good job. The gap is caused by their inability to create the expected outcomes. You will be working through an evaluation of your team later in the book. You will use that information to create a strategy that gets your team to where they need to be.

- **Limited Resources:** You should have already done an inventory of your infrastructures. Does your team have the time, efficient processes, supplies, equipment necessary to do their jobs well? If not, you will find yourself in the gap often.

- **Problem Employee(s):** I call it collateral damage. If you have problem employees who are allowed to remain in your employment you will be in the gap. Your other team members can not pick up all of the slack. Over time problem employees can create a negative culture as well.

So, what do you do about it if you are in the gap? As you look at the list above you will see that often eliminating the gap is in your control. Follow the steps we are outlining here for clear communication and holding your team accountable. The entire next section will cover the additional techniques you can use to decrease or eliminate your gaps.

Lead Well with a Focus on Celebration!

The next key to great leadership is to focus on celebration! Have fun! Focus on your successes and the successes of your staff. No matter how small. Remember, what you focus on expands. This is also true for others. Those behaviors that you call attention to tend to show up more often. Employees who are praised for success are much more likely to continue those behaviors that brought the praise.

The best way to keep a room full of people fired up and motivated is to have fun with it. Even serious missions based on healing those in painful and difficult situations are bolstered by a spirit of celebration.

It becomes easy with the daily grind to lose a sense of what we have accomplished and to fall back into our old habits. The best way to combat this is to actively pursue successes and to publicly celebrate them often. A spirit of celebration keeps the focus on the positive; it reminds you and your staff why you are here in a positive way. By pointing out good things, you are reinforcing those behaviors and values that should be encouraged. You are strengthening every individual's connection to your mission.

I will emphasize celebration in this book more than once because it is so important! In the context of this section, it is important to celebrate to help you maintain your laser focus on your progress and what has gone well. Choosing to be a person who celebrates will transform you into a leader who is always looking for celebration opportunities. Looking for reasons to celebrate will keep your focus where it needs to be, on success.

In my presentation, *Designing Drama Free Work* I show a great video called the Awareness Test. You may have seen it. If not, go to Youtube.com/user/kirsteneross. You can find it easily in my favorites list. It is called "Guerilla in the Midst." It is a video of two teams passing basketballs around. One team is in white t-shirts and one in black. Participants are asked to count the number of passes the white team makes during the video. People enthusiastically shout out numbers. They all want to be acknowledged for getting it right. But then, the announcer asks whether anyone has seen............ something else..............I don't want to give it away here. But rarely is there even one person in the room who has picked up on the something else. The scene is replayed and, once you are looking for the something else, it is so incredibly obvious that you cannot believe that it was actually there the first time. Often at least a couple people will want the entire video restarted to prove that it was there during the first viewing. There is always a lot of laughter as the realization hits that, yes, we really miss so much of what is going on when we are fully focused.

I love the video because it absolutely drives the point home that we must be intentional about where we put our focus or we will miss out on what is most important. If you feel like there is no reason to celebrate, it is likely that you are focusing elsewhere. Instead, you are choosing to focus on what is not right, what is left undone, what is out of your control and frustrating versus what you have accomplished, what has gone right.

I always envision people walking through a forest looking at the dirt-covered path. Their view of the forest from that perspective is not very good. Everything is black, there's not much to look at. But, as they shift their faces up towards the sun, suddenly there is greenery and sunlight, flowers and birds, color and light. That new, more positive perspective is just as close in your clinic.

Lead Well to Create a Culture

Now that you are feeling more empowered and are practicing the key traits of excellent leadership, let's put these skill to use to creating a great culture, your team machine. Every business has a culture, whether you are aware of it or not. It happens spontaneously or with intention depending on whether you put your focus there. And I highly recommend that *you* create it or your team will.

I cannot tell you the number of times I have heard, "All that people stuff is mamby pamby. I have more important things to do," "This is work. It's not supposed to be fun," "If they don't like it, there's the door," "I'll just get someone else in the position. I don't care," etc.

Creating a great culture is not about fun. Yes, a positive culture is more enjoyable, but ultimately, it is about creating an efficient team machine that positively affects your profits.

To get the most out of your team, you MUST pay close attention to their culture because it can make or break you. It goes beyond having the right people. Your team really does function like a machine. Many moving parts must work in harmony. One task leads to the next in a sequence. If your team machine is malfunctioning, your business is malfunctioning.

When you add people you are doing it to add more heads, arms and legs into the arsenal. Ideally, these other heads, arms and legs will be a coordinated extension of you as leader.

When you were young did you ever play that silly arm game? I wish I knew what it was actually called. In the game one person would stand straight with their arms behind their back while another stood behind with arms outstretched to become their arms. If you have children, maybe you have seen them play it. Often the person who is standing there will recite a play or sing a song. The person behind has to anticipate what they will do next so that they can make the appropriate arm and hand gestures. It rarely works. It always leads to tons of laughter as the person in back tries and tries unsuccessfully to anticipate what the next move should be.

This is funny in a child's game but if it is happening in your business it is frustrating and inefficient.

You can have all the right people with all the right attitudes but if the work environment is poor, the team performance will be poor. Bottom line.

Let's look at some examples that I have seen over and over with new clients:

- **Example #1:** A new employee is hired for her high energy and up-beat, positive attitude. You feel encouraged that she is exactly what your clinic needs to turn things around. The negativity will be a thing of the past once this little ray of sunshine hits the door. Then, three weeks in she is acting exactly like the rest of the team. What happened?
  - **Cause:** She was oriented to "Here's how things work around here." It is human nature to want to fit in. She was thrown to the wolves and it was sink or swim time.
  - **Diagnosis:** You cannot expect a new person in your

business to bear the responsibility of transforming an entire culture, especially if you expect that transformation to happen spontaneously. The expectation has not even been communicated to this employee. They are carrying the burden of your hope without knowing. They are also lacking the power of communicated leader support that is absolutely required to enact change in a culture. As leader you are most able to enact change. You can certainly enlist the support of members of your team but it must be done overtly and with a promise to support them as they do battle on your behalf.

- **Example #2:** A new employee is hired to do billing. She works there for 1 ½ years then goes out on a leave. Fellow employees take over only to find stacks and stacks of unprocessed paperwork representing thousands of dollars.
  - **Cause:** When she first started there was no training. She would ask questions but was always met with anger. She was treated as if she were stupid. She had a really good work ethic and wanted to do a good job but she really needed the paycheck and her ego couldn't take all of the criticism. She had been living with severe stress over the mounting backlog of paperwork and did not know what to do.
  - **Diagnosis:** The culture did not support training or open communication. Team members were actually hiding issues all over the place trying to avoid the wrath. The culture was so negative that the stress of doing less than standard work was easier to take than the stress of enduring the treatment for owning up to a mistake. Most of the energy was spent on "duck and cover" or "the blame

game" rather than on fixing problems or creating excellent patient service.

Now, I am not endorsing this behavior. Employees should still always do what is right. However, I *understand* the behavior. Even the best, most well intentioned people will go into survival mode and act in ways that they would not ordinarily.

I recently visited a chain store in the mall called "Buckle". The leaders in that organization have got creating a great culture down! Their employees were on fire with passion for denim and the coordinating items in that store. You could see a routine and feel the intentional focus on fun. They know their products, know how they will fit, which will work best for your body type, made suggestions for coordinating items, went out of their way to find shoes similar to what you'd wear the outfit with so you could put it all together or at least check the length. Multiple people made suggestions. They helped each other, and they spoke excitedly to each other about new items they had just gotten in.

Making that happen requires intentional focus. Their core values must support that culture, the hiring practices, training, how employees are rewarded and how they are led. They would never achieve this kind of culture accidentally and you won't either.

So, one of your most important roles as leader is to create a culture that supports your mission. And you have the power to do that if you aren't giving it away to your team. You create experiences that help to shape the beliefs of your team. Those experiences can be consistent with what you say is important or can work contrary to what you are trying to accomplish.

So for instance, you can say that you value input from your team. However, if their experience of you is that you ignore their input or get defensive when they provide feedback, the culture will be based on the latter. Future actions from your team will be to stay silent rather than risk voicing an opinion.

You have heard the saying that, "Actions speak louder than words." This is especially true here. As a leader, you will mold your business culture through the experiences you create for your team.

What you:

- Ignore,
- Tolerate,
- Focus on,
- Reward,
- Enjoy,
- Get angry over

all speak volumes to your team about what you actually value. Your team will take action based on the beliefs that they create. The resulting culture either will support you in your efforts or will stand in the way of making progress.

So, pay close attention to the experiences you are creating for your team. Work to make them align with the kind of culture you need to support your mission.

In these next sections, we will be working to build your culture!

<u>Catapult Task:</u> Leadership Transformation

I am creating these experiences that do not support the culture we need to meet my mission:

I commit to creating these experiences for my team so that our culture aligns with my mission:

I see these areas where I could improve my leadership style:

My leadership style is negatively impacting my clinic in these ways:

I commit to making these changes to my leadership style:

ᔆᕲᕟ

Section 2:
Engage Your Team

Coming together is a beginning, staying together is progress, and working together is success. ~Henry Ford

Now that you are fired up with passion and have a clear mission and vision for your practice and have learned the basics of great leadership, it is time to take the next steps. To make sure that your staff, both individually and collectively, is acting as a coordinated and impassioned extension of you. That the activity, energy, and full resources of the practice are all laser focused on your mission.

Unless you plan to run a tiny practice with a very localized mission, you cannot complete your important work as a lone ranger. To accomplish great work you must increase your circle of influence. You must focus your time and energy on utilizing your gifts while allowing others the opportunity to utilize their unique gifts in support of your mission as well. You need the impassioned support of an integrated, efficient team. A staff empowered to do their jobs. A staff equipped with the tools, processes, and resources they need to be successful.

As you move forward into the next chapters the tasks may get a bit harder for you. Know that all elements here are important pieces of the puzzle and many build from concepts you have learned in prior chapters. Unfortunately, there is no magic pill that makes this next series of steps smooth. You are entering a time of transition for you and your team. There will be hiccups, missteps, uncertainty, fear and frustration. Sometimes realizing that these are a normal part of the process is helpful. Do keep your eye on the prize! Do not let the discomfort of change derail you or your team.

～∂ ᶜ⌣

Fire Them Up!

*The mind is not a vessel to be filled,
but a fire to be kindled. ~ Plutarch*

You are fired up now let's get your team there! In this section, you will learn the specific steps required to create an impassioned call to action to share with a team that is empowered and working like a well-oiled machine.

Why do you want a fired up team? This is an important question because, as is the case in many instances in this book, we want to start with the why to help build your motivation for change.

Did you know that one of the tortures of war is doing physically demanding work for no purpose? Warlords had their prisoners spend entire days moving giant dirt piles from one side of a field to the other, back and forth. No specific outcome, no mission, no vision, no purpose.

It is not the tough work that is most difficult to bear. It is doing that kind of work with no goal to pursue. As humans, we have an innate desire to know that our lives have a purpose greater than ourselves. It is torture to feel like we are living lives like a hamster on a wheel, that all of our work is for nothing. Human beings fired up with passion will move mountains without hesitation. And they will feel good at the end of it, if they have a vision for the outcomes they are helping to create.

Do not let your workplace be a pile of dirt. Make sure that your employees know the value of what they are doing and why. How does each shovelful help you meet your bigger mission?

Help your team attach every task they do to the bigger mission. You want them to internalize your mission to elevate the importance of even the smallest duty.

Passion's Effect on Your Staff

Staff members who are fired up with passion feel that they are part of something bigger than they are, something more important than their own personal drama. They feel like a valued member of a team.

It becomes important to come to work everyday and they are given a reason to do the best possible job they can. When others on the team stand in the way, they seek to bring the team back on track. A staff that is wired for passion is efficient, hard working, and takes pride in what they accomplish every day.

Passion will motivate your staff to great achievements and will focus their energy towards a common goal.

An impassioned Team

- Achieves a 40% or higher performance than non-motivated employees
- Is 87% less likely to leave your organization
- Is loyal
- Has better morale
- Takes fewer days off
- Rises to the challenge
- Gets more done
- Creates bigger outcomes
- HAS LESS TIME FOR DRAMA!!

And it's not just about your team. When patients walk into a clinic that is driven by a common purpose, they immediately feel the difference. They feel supported and cared for. The staff is polite; things move smoothly. And when things don't go smoothly, there is a caring person ready to help, a staff member that is fully focused on being of service to the patient and that knows they have a team to back their efforts. Patients are able to relax and focus on their own healing because they are in a safe environment where others are truly interested in their care.

Negative dynamics, on the other hand, lead to stress, which has serious negative implications for you, your staff, your patients and your organization.

Staff members that are under damaging levels of stress exhibit the following behaviors and consequences for the organization:

- Carelessness and increased accidents
- Increase in sick days or personal vacation days
- High turnover rates
- Irritability and poor attitude
- Irrational behavior and difficulty with decision making
- Not motivated by work that they would otherwise be drawn to
- Increase in patient complaints
- Damage to the public image of the organization
- Increase in legal liability due to employee negligence

When your staff is engaged in a negative dynamic and is experiencing high levels of stress because of the work environment, there is a noticeable increase in mistakes and poor decisions. Staff members begin to cut corners on issues like patient confidentiality and bedside manner, either intentionally or unintentionally.

The American Institute of Stress estimates that organizational stress and the problems stemming from that stress siphons 20% of a company's payroll. Imagine what you could accomplish by eliminating this stress. You could hire additional nurses or support staff, give some much-needed raises, or update your facility.

Causes of Stress

Even more surprising and important than the effects of stress, is the cause of this type of stress. The same organizations that have researched the effects have also looked at the causes.

Organizational stress is most often caused by poor management and organization of the clinic. The way your clinic is organized is how jobs are structured. Take a moment to think about your clinic.

How many positions are there for each task?

How many responsibilities does each staff member have?

Are roles clearly defined?

Remember, we are all born with an innate desire to know that our lives have a purpose. Sometimes we are not consciously aware. Some people go through life with the feeling that there must be more. But they never stop to think about why or how they could change their life's direction by changing their perspective or taking some action.

We all have unique gifts that we are given to use in service to others. Those gifts may help others directly or they may be used in support of those who provide the direct impact. All are necessary. All are important.

Many people do not think of themselves, their talents, and their energy as a resource. It is important to do so. When you begin to think that way, you start to become more intentional about where you want to invest your gifts.

When I graduated from Michigan State's Masters Program, I became a highly sought after commodity. I was recruited by many large organizations. I decided that I must feel good about the company and the product or service they were providing. I made a conscious choice to turn down interviews with companies not aligned with my values. I felt like I had great talents to share and wanted to put my energy where I had passion. I ended up working in a health care setting. I was not directly involved in patient care, which is not my gifting. But I could help impact the work-life of those who were helping patients, and through them, I would could positively impact patients and help heal.

You need to help your staff do the same, if they haven't already. Even if they aren't directly involved in patient care, they still have an important role to play in allowing you to do what you do well. Help them identify their individual gifts, provide them with the resources to be successful, and attach them to your mission.

PASSION OVER FEAR

A second human truth is that we all have fear. We each have a section in our brain that functions to keep us safe. That part of the brain must work efficiently so it makes snap judgments. Anything determined to be new or unfamiliar is quickly identified as dangerous and something to be feared. As a result, we must learn to work around our fears constantly. No one is without fear. The outcomes in our lives are based on what we do with that fear. Some people let fear stop them in their tracks while others bust right through with little more than a glance.

You want your vision to be more compelling than your employee's fears. They will have them.

- Fear of failure
- Fear it won't work
- Fear of the unknown

- Fear of looking silly
- Fear of not being good enough
- Fear of what others might think

Give your team a great mission to work towards that will inspire them to bust through their fears and hurdle any barriers with ease. Give them the gift of tenacity with the energy of your vision.

So, we have covered the *"why"* to give you the motivation, now let's talk about *how* to get your team fired up!

Fire Them Up: Share Your Mission

So, share your mission. You want every employee to see it, read it, memorize it, and internalize it. Each member of your team must feel the importance of this statement. It isn't enough that they see it every day or even that they can recite it. They must feel passionate themselves about your goals. They will only develop that passion by first seeing it in you. You are their leader; they look to you for cues on what is important and what is not. You need to share your new mission statement with them in a way that conveys how meaningful it is to you and how they are part of it.

All of us want to be part of something bigger than ourselves; it is human nature. Make this the opportunity your staff has been looking for. Give them a reason to be better and to work harder. Give them a reason to come to work every day besides simply receiving a paycheck. When they feel your passion and know that they are part of your mission, they will want to come to work every day.

Share Your Mission: Let Them Feel It

You must share your mission with emotion. Passion is no more than 20% cerebral and 80% emotional. You cannot think your way to full passion. You cannot just send an email or hand everyone a piece of paper in a meeting. They need to FEEL your mission. Let your passion create contagious enthusiasm. Authentically share. Let them hear the excitement in your voice!

Begin at the beginning. When did you first discover this need in the world? Where were you? What did you experience as you felt that undeniable tug in your chest? What did you think? What will it feel like to make this positive impact in the world? Share some information from your Catapult Task *"Finding Your Original Passion."*

Be vulnerable and authentic with your team. Just tell it like it is, from the heart. That is what creates human connection. That energy will be transferred to your team.

Share Your Mission: Let Them See It

Post your mission for all to see. You should have it hanging visibly in your office, in the break room, in your clinic. Put it at the top of your written communications, have it in a frame during your staff meetings. Keep your mission at the forefront of everyone's mind. Make sure that your employees know why you are in practice. Keep everyone focused on the important difference you are making in the world.

Share Your Mission: Let Them Participate in It

Each staff member is a valuable resource and each needs to begin to see themselves that way. They have been given gifts to be used in the service of others. Your practice is where they will have the opportunity to fulfill their purpose.

Help your staff realize that they are important resources. You cannot do it without them. Create a mantra in your office, "We all help heal." Depending on the size of your practice, you may have staff members not directly involved in patient care. Left to their own assumptions, they may feel like their work is not as important. Each staff member needs to realize that he or she is an integral part of fulfilling your mission.

Take the time to brainstorm about how each task helps fulfill the bigger mission. Ask your team to think about the work they do and how they could each step up their game to help you accomplish your goals faster.

When I first started working on the presentation that this book is based on, I titled it, "Even Cleaning Toilets Can Be Fun." That title didn't stick, but I don't want to lose the importance of the concept. If you can attach even the smallest, most seemingly insignificant task to the huge impact you are making, then that small task is elevated in importance. The focused energy, the mindset, and the attention to detail, are all heightened to match.

The title, "Even Cleaning Toilets Can Be Fun" was actually inspired by a housekeeper in a health care setting. Years ago, I worked in Human Resources for Cottage Hospital in Grosse Pointe, Michigan. This particular housekeeper was always so friendly and enthusiastic.

I knew her job was tough and certain aspects of it, particularly in a hospital, could be quite disgusting. So, one day I asked her how she did it, how she stayed so upbeat and seemingly unaffected by the work she was doing. She said, "I don't really think about the actual work. I focus on the patients I am helping. I have empathy for them. I know that when a patient makes a particularly big mess (I won't get graphic about what she actually said here) I know that the patient must be feeling really, really bad. I focus on them and doing what I can to help them feel better. That way I never mind the work that I am doing no matter what."

See, she was not technically involved with patient care but she chose to see her work for how it could positively impact the patients. From there, she was able to maintain her enthusiasm for what could otherwise be a pretty thankless job.

Every task in your clinic can be similarly attached to your bigger mission. Help your staff begin to reframe their duties. Begin to speak about the positions and tasks in a new way.

Let's look at some examples of what a difference it can make when you elevate each job and task and speak about it in terms of the difference it can make towards meeting your mission.

Front Desk:

> **Current:** I answer phones, schedule appointments, and have patients fill out paperwork

> **Mission-Centered:** I create a welcoming environment for

people seeking to feel better. I make sure they are scheduled for their visits with us so that they receive all of the healing help that they require.

Biller

Current: I bill insurance companies by entering in the codes for the work we do.

Mission-Centered: I work to establish great relationships with our insurance representatives so that we receive appropriate pay with minimal delay for the work that we do. This keeps our doors open so that we can continue serving our patients.

Office Manager

Current: I handle all of the problems.

Mission-Centered: I take the administrative work from the doctor and maintain a smooth running office so that she can heal more patients.

Massage Therapist

Current: I do massages

Mission-Centered: I bring comfort to the patients' bodies so they can be more active in pursuing their own lives.

You get the picture. Have your team begin to attach their tasks to the bigger mission. Encourage them to be creative and have fun with the exercise of creating mission-centered job descriptions.

We will dive deeper into giving your team opportunities to participate in another section. For now, let's just focus on helping each member of your team see and feel the important role that they play in achieving your mission. This first section is about helping them learn to take personal ownership to internalize your mission.

<u>Catapult Task:</u> Mission-Centered Job Descriptions

Create a mission-centered job description for each position. Not necessarily a brand new official job description. Just have each staff member re-frame the significance of their job by attaching it to the bigger mission in 1 to 3 sentences.

♋◌⟋

Plug them In!

*The best executive is the one who has sense enough to
pick good men to do what he wants done, and self-restraint
to keep from meddling with them while they do it.*
- Theodore Roosevelt

Your employees are on fire for your mission. They have been inspired by your passion and have internalized it. Now, they want to participate and fulfill their purpose with you. Provide them with various opportunities to fully participate in your mission.

This means allowing them to have a voice. And having a voice doesn't mean just an opportunity to speak; it means the opportunity to be heard and a chance to see their ideas become reality. If you have rock stars on your team, and you'd better, they will have creative ideas to help serve your patients, to make the office run smoother, to make things more efficient, to provide better energy, to improve patient experience. Give them the opportunity to share their ideas and respond. Really listen, be appreciative, and implement the ideas that make sense. Many of them will.

Here are some basic strategies to allow your team to be ongoing, active participants in fulfilling your mission and vision.

Empower Your Team – Now Let them Work!

Once your staff is fired up around your mission you need to empower them to do their jobs well. In this section we will work on strategies you can use to do that well. Empowering your team begins with you. You must ensure that your staff members have the tools and the freedom, or autonomy, to do their best work.

Without autonomy, they are just working extensions of you. They will not have the freedom to find their own passion. Productivity will be stifled; it is time consuming to ask for permission for every little thing.

When I work with controlling leaders, I always picture the business as a giant helium balloon. The balloon represents the business that is trying to grow and soar. The micromanager is running from side to side trying to fill the balloon all alone, trying to tie off all of the loose ends. The balloon is not able to achieve its full potential. It simply is not a task that one individual can achieve. The true leader will give the team the freedom necessary to let the business expand.

Zappos.com, an online shoe store extraordinaire, provides a great illustration of a business providing excellent service through its people. The team at Zappos has the freedom to be creative in exceeding customer expectations. They can send cards, send a truck to pick up a shipment, deliver flowers, include a special gift in with a shipment of shoes. The team would not be as nimble if they had to ask permission for each little extra. Instead, the leaders leave these activities to the complete creative discretion of the team. The result is a fired up team providing awesome customer service and having fun while they do it.

Provide Autonomy

Give them the autonomy to conduct some of their work without your direct supervision. You can and should set boundaries around what they can do without you. If you have to be involved in every decision, your circle of influence is no greater than you. And your staff's ability to work quickly and creatively will be hampered if they have to wait for a conversation with you.

Create firm definitions if you are uncomfortable.

- Set a maximum price for purchases made without your approval.

- Give them space to handle an unhappy patient. By allowing your staff to provide a quick response, you can avoid escalated hurt feelings from the patient.

Difficulty in trusting your team can be about your shortcomings or theirs. In this section, you are going to do some analysis of your team members to determine whether they are currently able to effectively help you meet your mission. If not, you will create a game plan to get them there either with your current team or with some new players. Remember, you cannot do it all on your own. If you find there are issues with you, we'll work through that as well. Either way, you will be moving towards an increased circle of influence and more action towards your mission.

It probably goes without saying, but to empower your team does take courage as a leader and also trust. First, make sure they have the cornerstones of success in place. If the basics are not there, your delegation process cannot yield excellence. We will spend some time on each of the basic cornerstones of success. As always, though, you, as leader are ultimately responsible for correcting any shortfalls that you identify.

1. Knowledge, Skills and Abilities
2. Resources
3. Processes
4. Time

Assess Knowledge, Skills and Abilities (KSA's)

Do you know what knowledge, skills and abilities are required to be successful in each of the jobs you have in your clinic? Even if you don't have formal job descriptions (although you should) you still must have a basic understanding of what it takes to be a rock star in each position. Begin with the 1-3 sentence description your team completed in the last section if you have nothing else. Formalizing this step actually provides the building blocks for everything else that happens with your team. A job description, whether formal or basic will:

- Drive the hiring process. What will you look for during the interview process to identify that future superstar who will fit well in your organization?
- Determine what training is required at time of hire.
- Provide a standard for measuring performance.
- Help you create a performance-based compensation plan and a career path.
- Give you a basis for evaluating each employee's performance abilities and will help you identify where additional training resources must be utilized.
- Help you make a better decision about whether a new employee should continue employment beyond their introductory period.
- Allow you to evaluate your employees based on set standards.
- Give you the confidence to become an influential delegator.

Catapult Task: **KSA (Knowledge, Skills, Abilities) Analysis
Exercise 1 – The Jobs**

If you have an office manager, or someone who helps you with human resource tasks in your office, you can have them help you with this section.

If you have formal job descriptions for each position in your clinic, great! That is a nice starting point. Gather these and make copies so that you can write on them. If you don't have anything resembling a job description, you will have a bit more work to do.

Pick a job, any job, and take a fresh new look at the job description. Does it include all of the major tasks? If there is anything missing, add it.

If you do not have a job description, a great place to start is on the internet. Just do some Google searches for the position you are working on. You can also go to any of the main job search sights like careerbuilder.com or monster.com to see how your job has been described in a job posting. Or, you may want to bring in a trusted advisor. A Human Resource Coach or consultant probably will have worked on many job descriptions and would be able to help you create top notch, professional descriptions that really capture the essence of the job and meet any federal or state requirements.

Once you have all of the tasks down, take a fresh look at the training required to perform the tasks.

- Are there certifications or education mandated by either state or federal regulations?

- Are there education, training, certifications, classes that should be completed prior to hiring into your position?
- Is there training that must be satisfactorily completed in-house for your employee to meet the minimum qualifications?
- What temperaments or behaviors does a staff member have to have to be a rock star in the position?
- Do they need to be detail-oriented or customer service focused?
- Do they need to be flexible or follow strict guidelines?
- Do they need to be able to multitask and stay calm in a fast-paced environment or do you need a self-starter who will find things to do during inevitable downtime.
- What works best for your environment and culture?
- Who do they need to be to work well with you?

I have helped staff many clinics and it is important to get real about your own personality and quirks as a leader. If you are a fly by the seat of your pants, let it flow, tell you last minute, change your mind all the time kind of a leader, you are going to have conflict with a rigid employee.

You may need that person, though!

However, you will bump heads, so you must complete a self-evaluation to get real so that you can understand the conflict when it arises if you are hiring your opposite. And, you must let them know what they are up against during the interview process so that they can make an informed decision.

Or, maybe you don't want that kind of friction. You may only want fly by the seat of their pants employees. Just get real about it here.

You will need to complete this process for each job in your clinic. Even if you don't end up with a formal, final draft of a beautiful job description, you at least need the list of the minimum knowledge, skills and abilities required for success in each job. Remember to use language that attaches to your mission, while you are at it.

At some point, do plan to have good solid job descriptions that meet all requirements for federal regulations such as the Americans with Disabilities Act (ADA), for example.

⁓⊘⊙⁓

Catapult Task: KSA Analysis Exercise 2 - The People

Once you have completed the KSA analysis for each job, evaluate the person in each job. Please complete each of these steps. These are important building blocks to the next steps!

Again, you may want to have a trusted advisor help you. Or, if you have an office manager or other staff member who helps you with human resource functions you might have them assist. *A word of caution, though,* they must be mature enough to keep this process completely confidential. Furthermore, they must feel confident in their own abilities or be open to learning if they have room to grow in their own position. You need to be real with them as well. Do some reality checking here! I have been in many clinics where an office manager is a key to many of the problems with staff. The key to doing the exercise for maximum results is to get real and protect no one.

This is not about being vindictive or mean. It is about doing a reality check and making your patients the number one priority. You have big things to accomplish and you need the right staff functioning at their highest levels to create the biggest benefit for the world.

Did I hit a nerve? Were you cringing as you read that paragraph or did you feel defensive? If so, you may not want to bring your office manager in to this process. Even if you do not allow them to participate in their own evaluation, they will know that you are doing it. If they are open to critique and willing to grow into the position as it needs to exist in your new world then let them in. If they are defensive and unwilling to bend or change, you may want to keep this evaluation on the down-low. Call in a trusted advisor from the outside instead. Sometimes it is easier to get real when you have an unbiased outside party.

Do not worry; you are not going to make any final decisions yet. You are just starting to empower yourself by beginning to evaluate your options with your staff. The good news is it will be a winning situation for you regardless. You may have to navigate some tough decisions or actions to get there. On the other side is a full focus on passion and your mission. It's worth it!!

Catapult Task: Analyze the Team KSA's

Okay, enough pushing from me; use the form below to quickly document your initial thoughts about your staff.

1. Write down the name and job title of each member of your staff on a form like the one below or use an Excel spreadsheet.

2.

Employee Name	Job Title	KSA's	+, -, =	Action

3. Honestly and as objectively as possible, go through your list of employees one by one and compare their current level of knowledge, skills, and abilities to what is required of the position.

4. As you conduct this analysis, record where they excel and where they have shortfalls.

5. Where there are shortfalls, determine what is required for them to function at the level you need them to function. Is it training from an external source? Is it additional time shadowing a co-worker or do they maybe need an attitude adjustment? Be as specific as possible. What investment is required by you and by them?

6. Determine whether it is realistic for them to make the required changes. Are they willing? You may not know the answer to this yet. If you have not yet required them to function at an excellent level, if you've been allowing them to skate, allowing them to vent or cause drama, you do not necessarily know what they are fully capable of if the rules change or if a job is on the line. But, take a first best guess about whether or not it is doable.

7. If the answer is no, you do not feel that they can rise to the challenge of working to your new standards, the next question is, can they meet the exceptional standards of any of the other positions in your clinic? Maybe they are a real whiz at part of their job. There may be a way to restructure or move them to allow them to reach their full potential with you.

8. Perhaps, you have an employee or two who are doing very well in every aspect of their job. There may be an opportunity to provide them with some job enrichment or career advancement.

∽၈ఎ

The Rest of the Progress Equation

You should have already done at least some of the work of identifying where you stand in the areas of resources, processes and time. Go back to the Catapult Task you completed in the first section entitled "Assessing Your Infrastructures" You should have already thought through many of your processes and evaluated how they impact your ability to get work done, either positively or negatively. Now you will be looking more specifically at how these infrastructures impact your team's ability to work independently to be successful and also how they might impact the dynamics between people.

Resources

To be fully empowered to do their jobs your staff members need at least the basic resources. Do you have: equipment that works well, effective forms, phone systems, office supplies, space? You cannot gain full efficiency without the right resources. Take some time to evaluate your current resources. Make a list of any shortfalls. You can ask your team for input here. Do a cost-benefit analysis to determine the items in which you will invest.

Time

Does your team have the time to do their jobs well or are they always rushing to get everything done? There is a fine line between hitting your maximum productivity and overwhelming your staff completely. Are you realistic about what can be accomplished?

Processes

Is there a logical flow to your work or are you under constant chaos? Do you work around the same issues or errors day after day? Is there a good communication system? Where do you need to focus to gain additional efficiency? Create a list. Next we will discuss the additional steps in conducting a simple but effective process improvement process.

Process Improvement Initiative

Most people spend more time and energy going around problems than in trying to solve them. ~ Henry Ford

Improving processes that you have identified as problematic does not have to be difficult. In a nutshell, analyze your processes to make them work better. There are very complex systems for evaluating processes like Sig 6 but you do not need to get that technical. You can keep it very simple and still reap the rewards. At a minimum, begin by creating a list of issues, common errors, hiccups or barriers that impede your ability to reach goals. Once you have your list, allow your team to prioritize which issues they want to tackle first. I always recommend starting with a few that are easy to improve upon but have a big positive impact. I call it the "big bang for the buck" test. This gives your team some quick success and will motivate them to keep going. Carve out time weekly or monthly for staff participation. These activities are win – win – win! Your staff will have the opportunity to brainstorm improvements for your clinic. During that brainstorm they will get to know each other better. If you have a larger clinic with at least several different positions, it will give your employees the chance to learn more about what others do day to day. From that knowledge, will grow learning and understanding. They will also begin to see the larger picture of how other departments or employees effects their own jobs.

This knowledge, learning, and understanding lead to appreciation. They will begin to know each other, their coworkers' strengths, and their contributions. Your team will start to connect. They will get excited about the work they are doing. They will be united towards a common goal.

And, we haven't even gotten to the core outcome for which process improvement was designed yet, which is improving your clinic!! You will experience that as well! Work flow, patient flow, daily activities, charting, billing, any process you take on as a team will get better. Processes designed from a variety of perspectives are better! Each person in your clinic has a unique view of your systems. When you bring those views together and consider them before making a change, the result is beyond what one person can create. Your staff will also be more committed to consistently using the new processes because they played a part in creating the change. They have ownership in the design.

Additionally, you will have more reasons to celebrate as you become more and more efficient.

Have someone on your team who is a good organizer maintain a running list of the processes you will take on. That way you won't lose longer projects or ones that must be put on hold at first. It will also give you a quick visual of your successes. I usually highlight projects as they are completed so that the team can easily see that they are making progress. In those tougher times when you feel like nothing is getting done you can look back and say, "Wow, we've actually accomplished a lot!"

Here's an example of a table I use when I work with a team. You can easily create it in Word. Make sure this gets delegated to someone who will stay on top of it. Over time, the table will get quite large.

Start Date	Issue	Actions	Driver(s)	Doer(s)	Updates/ Notes
11/01	No consistent protocol for new equipment	~Create treatment protocols ~Train Docs ~Laminate bulleted version for quick reference	Dr. Smith and Office Manger	Dr. Smith, Office Manager and CA	Meeting scheduled for 12/05/2010
09/05/	Pt scheduling inefficient, double-booking	~test electronic scheduling software ~implement electronic scheduling calendar ~train staff	Office Manager	Staff	**DONE!**

Catapult Task: Analyze Team Resources

Let's get clear on whether your team has the tools to be successful. Again, start with the Catapult Task you completed earlier, "*Assessing Your Infrastructures*," and just look at it from a different perspective. You should already have a clear understanding about how your infrastructures impact your ability to get work done. Now look at them from the perspective of your team. Do poor processes or limited resources minimize your ability to delegate to your team? Or do they limit their ability to be successful?

What, if any, resource scarcities create a negative impact on your team?

What is the impact on your team or on your ability to delegate?

To what do you commit to enact change in this area? What process improvement initiatives will you engage in?

What processes limit your team's ability to succeed?

What is the impact of your inefficient processes on your team or on your ability to delegate?

To what do you commit to enact change in this area? What process improvement initiatives will you engage in?

Where is your team struggling with time?

What is the impact on your team or on your ability to delegate?

To what do you commit to enact change in this area? What process improvement initiatives will you engage in?

✨

Establish a Good Information Flow

Even in a fired up team a lack of communication can act like a sedative. "I can't move because I don't know what is going on!"

Great communication, on the contrary, provides a catalyst to activity.

"I know enough about what is going on and about our general direction to act independently at times with the assurance that my efforts will be well coordinated with the overall mission." Communication gives courage and empowers your team to work with precision.

Here are some basic strategies to implement to assure that you are keeping your team well informed and nimble.

Maintain a Good Meeting Rhythm

I cannot tell you the number of health organizations I have worked with where there is no consistent communication stream. I find frustrated owners and chaotic staff. There is no opportunity to hold staff truly accountable because there is no way to verify whether the employees actually knew what was going on in the clinic.

When your business is small, you and one other person, you can thrive on a communication process that consists of ad hoc conversations that you have in the hallway as you pass. However, once you get any larger than that, you need to invest some time in formalized communication streams.

I still believe that employees want to do a good job. However, in many of the clinics I have worked in, somehow the perfect storm was created – the wrong staff, failure to hold staff accountable or communicate clear expectations, tons of frustration and chaos all of which leads to a group norm of "It wasn't my fault." Employees begin to put energy towards making sure that they cannot be held accountable. Furthermore, the lack of communication supplies many avenues for hiding from accountability, "I didn't know", "I never heard about that", "I wasn't at the meeting", "she never told me." And the truth is you can't prove it because there is no documentation of communication.

Employee communication done well has the potential to:

- Encourage discretionary effort
- Reduce absenteeism
- Improve retention
- Increase efficiency

Providing clear direction will allow your staff to work with tenacity.

Your team wants to know where you are going, how you will get there, and what role they will each play in the journey.

Hold regular staff meetings with opportunity to communicate expectations and time to debate a bit. Remember, you have final authority. But really receive, hear, and consider input from your staff. This opportunity for give and take really enhances the feeling of your team being on a mission together.

Assign accountability for communication to your leader(s). The office manager could be accountable for all communication. Or you may have separate communication accountability between doctors. Communication, like all other important tasks, must be assigned to specific people so the ball is not dropped.

Create a system for communication that works. Utilize the system consistently.

- An email blast
- Alerts posted in a specific spot
- Memos in mailboxes
- A communication log

Team Huddle

The huddle is just another name for a quick, informal meeting. I am sure that the name derived from the football huddle that happens between plays. In football the huddle gives the team the opportunity to come together quickly to gain focus, create a strategy, and evaluate how the last play went. The quarter back also passes on information received from the coach.

This is exactly what your team huddle should accomplish. It is a chance for your team to come together discuss what could have gone better from the day before, communicate about any specific patient issues, processes that need a tweak and to pass on information from you their leader, either directly from you or indirectly from an office manager.

At least once a day, your team should have a huddle where employees can engage in quick problem solving and communicate systems that need work. Discuss any special circumstances for the upcoming day; communicate anything new, talk about business goals (patient visits, reactivated, new patients), marketing strategies, list process improvement needs. Start the day on a positive note and with an opportunity for good communication.

Weekly Staff Meetings

Make sure to allow time for good, effective staff meetings. You should have at least one every other week, though once per week is better. I am never a proponent of having a meeting just to have a meeting. If you have meetings but they are not effective they are a complete waste of time. The answer is not to stop having meetings, though. On the contrary, commit to having the meetings and then run them well so that they are effective. Make them a priority. Tell your team that they must be on time and you do the same if you will be in attendance. Assure that meetings start and end on time and that idol chit chat is kept to a minimum.

Team Meeting Topics:

Here are some key topics to incorporate into your meeting agendas to assure that you are using your time well:

- **Allow time for education of staff by staff**: Every clinic I've worked with has the constant need to train team members. Whether it's new processes or regulations, new initiatives or just keeping up with certifications, there is always something new to learn.

   Have you ever heard that the best way to learn is to teach? If you want members of your team to really excel, give them the opportunity to teach other staff members. It saves you the time, gives them the motivation to really learn what they will teach, provides an opportunity to work a new muscle and take on a new challenge, and is a great way for your other team members to learn. If your staff meetings have morphed into the "You Show," trust me, they will welcome the opportunity to hear from their peers. It's a win – win – win!

- **Create time for process improvements:** The weekly staff meeting is the perfect time to create issues lists that will become process improvement initiatives. You will not conduct much problem solving during the meeting. Rather, focus on assigning responsibilities and communicating updates. This item should be included on every agenda.

- **Discuss business goals:** Your team wants to participate in your mission and the key purpose of your staff meetings it to communicate direction and success. Take the time to share any business goals that you are working towards. Ideally, you will have some key measures that can be discussed weekly to determine progress. For instance, do you monitor weekly patient visits or new patients? Let them know where you are so that they can help come up with ideas to help you meet or exceed your goals. And, when you do that, make sure to take some time to celebrate!

- **Brainstorm marketing ideas:** I love to encourage my clients to include all team members in marketing strategies. At a minimum, they could be handing out business cards to people they know to educate their network about the services you provide. Word of mouth is the best form of advertising and you should be taking full advantage.

- Encourage them to get creative about other strategies to educate the public about your offerings. You have great services to provide and there are many people who could benefit. They can't benefit if they don't know. Have them help you get the word out. Make it a part of everyone's job.

- Of course, there will be some circumstances where marketing by word of mouth is not appropriate. Perhaps your team can help you come up with new ideas to establish relationships with other clinics who offer related services.

- **Assign tasks and give deadlines:** I am not a big proponent of solving problems in the meetings but you should definitely assign responsibilities and give deadlines for problem solving during the meetings. The real work happens outside the meetings with key players only. There is no need to monopolize the time of your entire team if only a few need to be involved.

- **Design an interactive meeting that involves communication in both directions:** This is a key goal of any meeting. Provide time for communication in both directions on the topics listed above and any others that are relevant. Meetings are for interaction and should be only part lecture.

Here is a meeting outline used in a chiropractic office that I worked with years ago. It has been very instrumental in changing the structure of their meetings, which are now very interactive and focused on the key goals of the clinic only.

Inspiration

- Acknowledgement,
- Quotes,
- Mission Statement
- Review

Review Chiropractic Statistics

- Patient Visits
- New Patients
- Report of Findings

- Rescans
- Rescheduled Rescans
- Missed or Cancelled Rescans
- Totals Last Week
- Project Visits this week

Service Totals

- Hydrobed
- Massages
- Yoga Participants
- Suppliments

Review of Upcoming Workshops and Marketing Initiatives

1.

2.

3.

New Patient Review (doctor to discuss & review needs & expectations)

1.

2.

3.

4.

Recalls & Reactivations (people who you called back or who we should call to reactivate)

Challenges or Issues and Solutions

Date of Upcoming Departmental Meetings Schedule or REQUEST FOR MEETING

Task Manager

Task/Action Item

Responsible Member

Due Date

Complete Date

Updates

Solution-Centered Communication

As you begin to encourage more and more communication, you want to make sure that your team meetings never morph into complaint sessions either. I have seen far too many cultures support whining. If there are issues to discuss, the items should be documented and then someone needs to take ownership of fixing each item on the list.

I like to have my clients use a "Gripe and Grumble Form". A sample is below. They work well because they emphasize the solution, not just the complaint. The easiest part of the improvement process is pointing out the flaws. The real meat is in coming up with solutions. Employees have a tendency to modify their complaints accordingly if they are required to provide solutions as well. They will make sure that it is worth the effort.

Here is the sample Gripe and Grumble Form. Put your logo on the top and you can fit two to a page.

Turn a Gripe or a Grumble into a Request or a Solution

It's easy to complain, gripe or grumble. But it takes energy without getting you anywhere. And, you end up sucking energy from those around you.

If your gripe or grumble is worth spending any energy on, then it's worth a bit of time and energy to fix it. If it's not worth your energy to fix it, then it's not worth your energy to gripe about.

If you have a gripe or grumble that is worthy, fill out the form, come up with a solution or request and give it to the office manager. Either way, get it off your chest!

Gripe/Grumble:

Request/Solution:

Catapult Task: Communication Strategies

I have identified these issues with our current communication:

Our communication shortfalls result in these issues:

I will make these changes to our staff meetings:

I commit to these changes to improve communication:

⚘

Communicate Clear Expectations

If you just communicate you can get by.
But if you skillfully communicate,
you can work miracles. ~ Jim Rohn

Ultimately it's all about making sure that your team is working in concert with your goals and objectives. This can mean documenting everything from huge initiatives as a goal or expectation to the smallest rule about cell phone use. Your employees can feel more confident if they know where the boundaries are. And you can feel more confident if you have some!

We will begin very simply with the basics of why you should have a complete policy manual and what should be included in an attendance policy. We will then discuss additional strategies for assuring that you are communicating clear expectations that are aligned with your mission and vision. The goal is to know that each individual on your team has a clear sense of how they can make an impact and what they are accountable for personally.

Your team must have a clear understanding about what is expected of them so that you can hold them accountable.

Policy Manual

When my two boys were little we frequented the local fast food play places with friends. It gets cold and snowy during the winter in Michigan so you need a good indoor spot to release little boy energy!

At the end of each play date the following would occur: I would say, "Come on boys. Time to go." They would stop what they were doing immediately, walk directly to me and say, "Thank you for taking me."

Jaws dropped and eyes popped in amazement. I often had moms ask, "How did you get them to do that?"

My secret: I set the expectations up front and told them the consequences. They knew that the four golden rules for getting to come back were:

1. Finish eating your lunch
2. Play nice
3. No whining when it was time to leave
4. Thank mom for bringing you.

They knew that if they did not follow these rules the consequence would be no play place for a long time. And I was a mom who followed through with consequences so they were not going to chance it.

Your policy manual is no different. Even if you have just one employee you should have a basic policy manual for your office. It provides a simple mechanism for communicating what it takes to be successful in your environment. At a minimum, it should cover expectations around topics such as: cell phone use, internet access, attendance, smoking, dress codes. It should also spell out the specific consequences of failure to comply such as the type of discipline you will engage in.

Remember, your team wants to do a good job. You are the one who will define what doing a good job looks like. Start with the basics first. Then define what it means to do a good job for each position.

Attendance Policy:

I will go into further detail on this one. A good attendance policy is a must. Too often, attendance becomes an issue for employees and a source of resentments among team members. Clearly spell out a rule for the number of times an employee can be absent and how often he or she can be tardy and, as always, communicate the consequences for failure to comply. Doing this will give your team the opportunity to choose well. (We will be covering a good discipline process later)

A good policy provides for a reasonable number of absences and some tardiness. Life does happen. If you structure it well you do not have to get into the game of determining whether the excuse was legitimate. All excuses have equal weight. No subjectivity.

Here are my recommendations for structuring a sound Attendance Policy. Of course, check to make sure it is compliance with any laws or regulations in your area.

Regular Attendance and Punctuality

It is important to come to work on time and regularly. You depend on each individual employee to be present for work as scheduled. That said, circumstances will arise that make being absent or late for work unavoidable. That is understandable and acceptable. However, excessive or repeated absenteeism or tardiness is not.

Types of Tardiness

The most common type of tardiness is being late to work. However, I also recommend including returning to work late from breaks or leaving early as a tardy as well. Being "on time" means being at your work area and ready to begin work, not just being in the building or at the time clock.

Limits on Absenteeism and Tardiness

Monitor your attendance if you don't already. Or, if you have a report you can run from your time tracking system, do it now, just for the heck of it. Do you have some attendance issues you were not aware of? If you do not set timely arrival as a standard you generally do have people who routinely come in late. And it is usually the same people.

You should base your attendance/punctuality standards on an occurrence system. Any period of unscheduled absence, regardless of length or reason, results in one occurrence. If an employee is sick for three consecutive days, require a physician's note verifying their illness and documenting that they are able to return to work.

A conditional grace period of ten minutes or less for tardiness can be established to allow for infrequent, unexpected delays in reporting to work at the start of the shift. Abuse of the grace period should cause this privilege to be suspended.

If an employee is tardy more than ten minutes but less than 30 minutes, it should result in one-half of an occurrence. If an employee is tardy by 30 minutes or more, it should result in a full occurrence.

I recommend issuing discipline as defined below:

- Three occurrences in any 30 day period
- Four occurrences in any 90 day period
- Seven occurrences in any six month period.

If an employee works a reduced schedule, the occurrences should be prorated.

The level of discipline an employee receives for violation of the absenteeism or tardiness policy should be determined by the step they are on in the progressive discipline process. Written warnings are considered active for purposes of progressive discipline for a period of 12 months. For example, if the employee's written warning was issued July 1 of this year, the 12 month period runs through June 30 of the following year. Any combination of three written warnings in a 12-month period shall be cause for termination.

Make sure that your employees know that the intent of the policy is not to create a "right" to a given amount of time-off on a regular basis regardless of actual need.

Catapult Task: **Policy Manual**

I commit to documenting and formalizing our unwritten office rules:

I see these areas where it would be helpful to have established guidelines:

I will utilize an attendance policy consistently:

Master the Art of Great Delegation

It sounds so simple; just tell people what to do. But, many leaders struggle in this area. It's hard to relinquish control. Many times, leaders I work with feel discouraged because they don't get the results they want when they ask staff to perform a task. Too often, they decide it is easier to do it themselves.

The problem is that this sets a precedent with the staff. "I don't need to do a thorough job. My boss takes over and finishes anyway." Or, "My boss double checks it anyway. I don't really need to worry about getting it right." Or, worse yet, "Why bother starting it? She ends up taking it back and doing it anyway. I'll just wait for that to happen rather than waste my time."

If you have kids, you already know this phenomenon. If you ask your child to do something three times and then start yelling at them to get moving and this is your pattern, you have taught your child to move only when you start yelling. Or, you tell your child no and they start to whine, then cry, and then throw themselves on the floor. If you give up and give them what they want at this point, they have learned that the quicker they throw themselves on the floor, the quicker they get what they want.

You've heard it before, "We teach people how to treat us." Even when you have the best of intentions, you can end up creating an ineffective culture. And, if this is how you are operating your practice, your staff members are frustrated and feel mistrusted, while you are angry and overwhelmed.

I always assume that people want to do a good job and like feeling that they are. If you are not allowing your staff to function at their highest potential you are robbing them of the opportunity to feel fully successful. Employees who are not able to feel successful end up feeling frustrated and resentful, not the optimum emotions for a great working environment. Delegating work that stretches the capabilities of your staff will catapult their success, fire them up, and will create an environment where excellence is the standard.

You need to create a culture where your staff members feel accountable for their work and have opportunity to excel. You also want to foster a no-excuses or just-get-it-done mentality. And, like everything else we've been talking about, it begins with you. You need to do some reality checking to see what part you are playing in creating a culture where it is acceptable to give it less than your all.

The good news is delegating is a simple process. And, if it's a struggle for you to delegate, I am sure you are missing just one of the important steps. Every leader I've ever worked with, and there are many, has been missing at least one of these key elements. It is usually possible to transform your delegation style with a small tweak though.

The goal is to delegate well and then let go. We will go over the simple steps to take. If you are already starting to feel a panic attack coming on or are thinking that the entire clinic will fall down in shambles if you let go of your activities, don't worry. We'll create a step-by-step process that allows you to take only small steps, if necessary to get where you ultimately need to be. You can start practicing these steps with some teeny, tiny activities. If you follow each step correctly, you will experience success. Take note of that success and then delegate some bigger, more important tasks. As you feel success with those, delegate bigger tasks and projects. Before you know it you will be confidently delegating tasks left and right.

Here are the important steps in order:

What

Take time to get clear about what you are delegating so you can succinctly communicate it to your staff.

- Specifically what is it that you will delegate?
- Is it an entire project or is it a task?
- Where does this fit in the scope of your practice?
- What outcome will it create?
- What difference do you need to see?
- What standard of quality needs to be met?

Who

Select one staff member who will be 100% accountable for making sure that this task or project gets completed. They may not be the only one working on it. As a matter of fact, they may not actually do any of the work. But, by delegating to this person, he or she is fully accountable for ensuring that it is done on time and correctly. And ultimately, this is what you want. If multiple people are accountable, there is too much opportunity for finger pointing or passing the buck, "I thought she was going to do it."

Sending a blanket delegation to your staff is like a bride throwing a bouquet. You don't want to turn your back, close your eyes and toss. You are leaving it to chance that someone will catch it and go. Sometimes this works, but more often it just falls to the floor. Instead, you want to treat delegation like the Olympic Torch runner. You want to pass the task to one person who will be a good steward of the responsibility. And once passed, you must let go. The last torch runner does not run alongside or continue to hold on. They pass it and stop. Go on to the next thing.

I always use the term, "moving it off your plate." And that is the goal. We want to completely take the task or project off your plate and out of your brain space. You must completely let go. If you are still worrying, brainstorming, considering, or anything else with regard to a task or project you have delegated, then you have not let it go. Ultimately, you are leaving yourself accountable. It's still on your plate and your staff knows it. You cannot create a new culture without changing yourself. Begin now.

If you are thinking that there is no one on your staff qualified to take on this project or task then it is time to do some reality checking. Really? You are truly the only one capable? Have you made poor hiring choices or have you failed to invest in appropriate training? Because, once again, it all comes back to you. The answer can no longer be, "They can't do it."

Now is the time to fix it either by:

- Changing your mindset, immediately or over time
- Training existing staff based on the Catapult Task you completed earlier

- Starting from scratch

Your success depends on your ability to trust your team members. The Lone Ranger cannot accomplish as much as a general with a platoon of soldiers.

How (Optional)

This portion is optional. If you are delegating to a seasoned staff member, they may already know how to do the job. It might come off as condescending for you to provide the step-by-step instructions. However, if you are delegating to someone new to the work it may be necessary to provide some detail. Where will they get the information? What phone numbers will they need to call?

Remember, the ultimate goal of great delegation is getting the job done efficiently and done right.

Unfortunately, I have seen some leaders who get a kick out of watching their staff struggle with a project. Sometimes it's an ego thing. If this is you, it is not effective! You are letting your ego win and your practice lose.

By When

Make sure to communicate a specific deadline. Giving a task and saying, "Get this done when you can" does NOT communicate a sense of urgency. If you are delegating with this kind of language no wonder you are feeling frustrated. "When you get a chance," usually does not happen. You may intend to be nice or to acknowledge that your employee is busy. Or maybe you really want them to prioritize the work themselves. Ultimately, though, what they are hearing is, this is not a big deal." And you end up feeling like you can't delegate anything because your stuff never gets done.

If you are delegating a larger project, create some intermediate deadlines along with the final deadline.

Create a Communication Schedule

This is one of the most often missed steps in the delegation process. And it is a very important, especially as you work to build your delegation muscle. When you delegate the task and deadline you must also create a communication loop by requesting that the delegate provide you with updates at specific intervals.

You want to offload this part of the process. If you don't, you have not fully delegated because you end up creating this scenario: On Monday, you ask someone to do a project. You tell them the deadline is one week from this Thursday. By Friday, you will begin thinking to yourself, "I wonder how they are doing on that project? Man, I really hope that they get it done on time. If they don't, it will really mess up ….fill in the blank" You begin to think and worry about it more and more. Finally, you go to your employee to ask them, "How is that project coming?"

The problem is two-fold. One, you are still taking up your brainspace thinking about the project. You have not fully offloaded it. You still actually own it. Your energy is still being used on this project.

Two, when you constantly go to your employees to ask or remind, you are setting a precedent that they don't need to worry about the project when you delegate it because you will remind them and may even offer assistance. In this scenario, they are not motivated towards excellence.

As an alternative, tell your delegate, "The project is due a week from this Thursday. By Friday, I want you to send me an email detailing the progress you have made. On Tuesday, we will sit down for 15 minutes to cover where you are and any support you need from me or other staff members."

Now, you can sit back and relax knowing that the employee is fully accountable for the project and for providing you with updates. You do not need to ask. They have fully taken on the responsibility.

When you first start to delegate this way it may feel very uncomfortable to let go and wait for updates. If this is the case, don't give up. Just take a smaller step. Make the intervals between updates shorter. If you need an update daily, set that as the standard. Slowly you will build confidence in yourself and in your staff. The more success you experience with delegating the easier it will become. Soon you will be delegating and requesting very few updates. You will have set the stage for an environment where your staff is fully accountable immediately and you are comfortable and confident in their abilities.

Offer Your Support Up Front

As part of your No Excuses campaign, you must offer support up front and then let it go.

Make it very clear that an excuse like, "I couldn't get it done. I didn't have time", will not fly. The employee accountable for the project must inform someone if he or she is falling behind and must ask for assistance. Assistance can come from you, if it is initiated by the delegate.

What to Delegate

One of the privileges of leadership is being able to delegate what you do not want to do. But don't just take advantage of it because you can, take advantage because it's a smart business decision. We all have gifts we are born with. I like to think of them as God-given talents. We should be spending at least 80% of our time on the areas of our gifting. The rest, if possible, should be delegated to others. You have people in your clinic who have gifts that are complimentary to yours. Doesn't it make sense to allow them to do things they are best at too?

Think about tasks that you do on a routine basis now that are a struggle. They zap your energy or you might employ creative procrastination techniques to avoid doing them. These are key tasks to focus on as you create your delegation list.

Catapult Task: Commitment to Delegate

These tasks zap my energy and take me away from what I do best:

I am not very good at these tasks. Others do them much better than me:

I have these resources available to delegate to (include team members, trusted advisors, and service providers):

I commit to delegating these tasks to these specific people:

I will get out of my comfort zone at least 3 times in the next week to delegate more:

I commit to using all the key steps to the delegation process:

I have had these successes:

⌒♈⌒

Barriers to Great Delegation and How to Hurdle Them

If you are following the steps above but still find that the delegating is not creating the results you want, it may be a result of one of these common barriers. Identify the issue so that you can fix it. Because saying, "I'll just do it myself" is not the right answer! You only have so much capacity, period. If you are trying to do it all your circle of influence in the world is smaller than it could be and you are probably very overwhelmed. It is time to do some reality checking again.

Below are some of the more predominant barriers to delegation with actions you can take to hurdle them:

Your Control Issues: You have a fear of letting go. You feel like you must provide your input or everything will go awry. You have to know what's going on.

> **What it looks like:** You constantly ask staff what they are doing. You want to know details that really don't matter. You are unable to give your team the autonomy to complete even the smallest task or make even the smallest decision without your input.

Even when you delegate a task, you end up taking it back or jumping in to rescue. Fear grips you if you don't. Your staff members may not even start projects you delegate because, why bother?

Or you hire a professional and then proceed to tell them exactly how to do their job. Require them to do what you've done in the past. You end up with no change because you are limiting them to your knowledge base rather than tapping into theirs. Then you feel frustrated because you are paying for someone who is not adding value.

What it feels like: You feel overwhelmed and your staff feels mistrusted and frustrated.

What you can do: Start slowly. Pick some very small tasks in the office and follow the delegation steps diligently. Do not step in, no matter what. Bite your tongue; sit on your hands. Do whatever it takes. And when your staff completes the task, take note. Start creating a mental list of successes in your head or even on paper. As the list of successes grows, so will your confidence. You can let go! Things will get accomplished without you. You will start to feel some freedom from your fear and will enjoy spending more time in your passion. Begin to delegate bigger and bigger tasks. Then move to larger projects. Each success is a step in the right direction. As always, celebrate your progress!

Perfectionism: You envision one specific way that things should be done and one specific outcome, regardless of the task or project. There is no wiggle room, one way or no way. You cannot let go because they might not do it exactly as you would. While excellence should be the standard sometimes there are multiple ways to reach it. Perfection is not realistic and is often the culprit of control issues. I always think of the mom who complains that she has to do all of the laundry because no one will fold the towels the way she wants. She stays stuck folding towels while her kids miss out on the opportunity to feel responsible and learn a life skill.

What it looks like: Nothing is ever good enough. You feel like your team members are inept because they don't meet your standards, but you can't ever get there either. Something is always wrong. You are always jumping in to take over.

What it feels like: Fear is the result. Fear that things will not be good enough and frustration that no one can get there. Blame. Your staff feels paralyzed and frustrated. They can't do anything well enough, why bother? You feel overwhelmed because more falls on your shoulders. And you feel frustrated because nothing is ever right.

What you can do: Perfectionism can be a tough one to let go. There are often many layers of fear that create the phenomenon. Fear of making a mistake, fear of letting people down or disappointing them, fear of everything falling apart. Perfectionists often "what if" their lives away. To work around this one, you just HAVE to start practicing letting go. Perfect standards are not realistic. You'll white knuckle it initially. But let your team complete a project or call something finished yourself before it is perfect. Sit back and wait for what will come. Rarely will the outcome be as bad as what you envisioned. Often, there will be no negative fallout at all! Sometimes, unbelievably, your team will come up with something BETTER than what you had envisioned!

As you experience mini successes, store them for ready access in your brain database or keep a list. These successes will build and as they do you'll feel more confident in just letting go. Slowly allow bigger and bigger tasks to be complete. Allow your team to take on bigger projects. Allow them the freedom to do it their way. Continue to grow that list of successes. Eventually, you will be getting a lot more done and feeling a lot less stress! Trust me on this! I've helped many leaders with this one and it IS better.

You have the right staff but they have not been properly trained: You've done the reality checking. It is not that you are afraid to delegate. Your team members really do NOT have the skills to complete the work that you need done. They are willing and want to help, they work well together, and they have good positive attitudes and the ability to learn. You just have not allotted the time required for you or another team member to train them.

> **What it looks like:** You are doing all the work or some things just are not getting done because no one has the skills to do it. It looks like all the best intentions without any of the desired results.

> **What it feels like:** You are not as productive as you could be and neither is your staff. It feels like constant barriers to getting things done. Your staff is frustrated because they believe in your mission and want to help. They just aren't able to help as much as they would like.

What you can do: Get them trained. Take a step-by-step approach. Work through the list you created in the earlier section when you evaluated your staff based on the required KSA's. Prioritize the list by the training that is most necessary and figure out a way to get it done. Do it yourself or send them out to get the knowledge that they need. If you have great staff members then you want to invest in their success. Great staff members eventually burn out if they don't feel successful. And they cannot feel successful if they do not have the skills to do their jobs well.

You don't have the right staff: You've done the reality checking and it's not your fears or control issues that stops you from delegating. You have done a thorough job with the checklist in the previous section and have found that you just do not have the right team in place. You cannot delegate because they cannot do the work. Maybe you have provided the right training and they just don't get it. Or maybe they are missing that heart to serve and do not have the ability to care about your patients the way you need them to. They are unable to see what needs to be done or to take the initiative. Or maybe they are defensive and just don't want to take anything new on.

What it looks like: Chaos. You tell your staff to do something. They don't respond. Or, maybe, you are to the point where you won't even try to ask for anything to avoid the attitudes. You are a lone ranger in a sea of staff. There is little coordination between you and them. They just do their own thing and you try to avoid contact. Or you ask for things and are ignored or experience conflict.

What it feels like: It feels like you have no power in your clinic. You are frustrated and resentful. Your staff members realize either they are wrong and worry, or they don't care and act defensive. If they can maintain control, their jobs are safe.

What you can do: Take back your power! You might want to skip ahead in the book to the next section. The steps there will help you begin weeding out employees who are not willing or able to help you move towards your mission. Right now, you are investing in barriers. Paying them is not money well spent. You could be spending the same money on rock stars who would help catapult your progress. Wait until you get to that chapter, or do it now. But know that the weed out process is coming.

In the meantime, at a minimum, please, do not accept defensiveness. Do not feel afraid or walk on eggshells in your own business. Take baby steps if you must. Do begin to stand up for yourself, your patients and your mission. Delegate something very small and just walk away. Follow all of the steps in the process. Maybe you will be surprised. If they don't do it, say something. Delegate it again. Begin to give consequences for failure to act. (Again, see the next section.)

Your staff does not take responsibility: You delegate tasks and your employees just shrug their shoulders and say they do not have time. Or, maybe they don't even acknowledge hearing you.

What it looks like: Deer in headlights. Everyone looks at you with a blank stare. They have no idea what you are talking about. Or they give you 101 reasons why they couldn't get it done, all with no emotion at all. They either don't care or don't feel like the task was important at all.

What it feels like: It feels like you are the only one who cares about anything. You have to do it or it won't get done. You are misunderstood or not heard. They have an alternate agenda that you are not aware of that runs contrary to your vision.

What you can do: Make sure that you are delegating each task to one specific person. Be especially clear about deadlines and communication timelines to create that call to action. Let them know that they are fully accountable and there are no excuses. If at first you get no response, utilize your discipline process, which is covered later in this book. It won't take long before your staff realizes you are serious.

You are reluctant to give your team more work: You feel like your staff is already too busy. You feel bad for them, so you continue to take on more and more and more. You don't want them to feel overwhelmed or overworked. You want them to like their job. Or, maybe they are really too busy.

What it looks like: You are totally stressed out, overworked and overwhelmed. They are either aware or not. Perhaps they could do more, but think you don't want them to. Or, maybe they don't realize how overworked you are.

What it feels like: It feels like you have no time for the work you were born to do. You may feel resentful of your team because you feel overwhelmed and they have time to relax. You wish they would jump in but they don't.

What you can do: Do some reality checking again. Could they take more on? Perhaps their productivity would increase with more work. They may even enjoy the new challenge. If they are actually busy, can you look at some process improvement initiatives? What are you doing that could be done more efficiently? Where can you streamline process? What activities could be minimized or eliminated? Is there anything that could be outsourced? Can you add any additional staff?

Staff attitudes – defensiveness, rudeness, anger, frustration, hostility: Some negative emotions are legitimate. Maybe you know you aren't a great boss or that the constant need to put out fires has left your staff frustrated. You empathize with them. However, even when feelings are legitimate or have an obvious root cause, there is a professional and appropriate way to communicate those feelings.

Other attitudes like defensiveness, rudeness, or hostility, have no place in your clinic. These are just grown-up versions of temper tantrums used to maintain control. Staff members with these attitudes are working to get their way. They are not thinking about your patients.

Your patients are picking up on this negative energy and it is bringing you down. The focus is on the attitudes rather than on the mission.

What it looks like: It looks like temper tantrums and immaturity.

What it feels like: It feels like terrible negative energy. It feels like power struggles. It feels like poor communication. If your staff is getting away with this, you are either turning a blind eye and trying to avoid it or are bobbing and weaving to their whims. They would not continue to act this way if it wasn't working.

What you can do: You cannot tolerate negative attitudes in your clinic. Period! Your patients are coming in to be healed. They don't feel good. They do not need a zap of negative energy on top of it. And, trust me, they are feeling it or, worse yet, may be experiencing it! Many will not tell you. They will just vote with their feet! Or, perhaps they will tell their friends, "I love my doc but I just can't stand the front desk. They are so rude! It feels like I am an inconvenience when I come in." And, with social media sites like Facebook and Twitter readily available, people can communicate their feelings to a large audience very quickly. Not the kind of press you want for your business!

Now I KNOW this is not the experience you want for your patients. But, reality check time, if you are allowing negative attitudes this is their experience! Your staff is an extension of you, for good or bad. They are a major part of the entire patient experience.

I could go on and on here but will save it for the later chapter when we cover this topic in detail. But this one really gets me!

In the mean time, I will say, be the kind of leader you must be to remove the negativity from your clinic. When I work with a team exhibiting negative energy I just flat out tell them that it will no longer be tolerated. I teach them about assertive communication. That becomes the new standard. You speak with your mouth, at an appropriate time, with appropriate words, tone, and speed of speech. You use good, positive body language. You respect one another.

When you set out clear expectations for behavior, your team then has a choice to make. They will either choose to act like a grown-up who is focused on your patients or will choose to continue to act like a three-year old. They are empowered to do the right thing or not. It's their choice, their consequence.

Unfortunately, defensive staff members find it very difficult to change. A defensive attitude creates a wall that blocks information about change. Often, these staff members must go. Give them the opportunity to be successful by clearly communicating the expectation. You can always hire a coach to come in and help you if you need the assistance. Just do something about it. You must!

You are constantly putting out fires: You have not taken the time to get ahead of the game. You are not organized, so you cannot plan. There is no time to be an effective delegator because you do not think about projects or tasks until you are on top of the deadline. Or, maybe you are an adrenaline junkie who thrives on a deadline. You are subconsciously creating scenarios where you must rush and barely make it.

> **What it looks like:** Chaos. Day to day operation is prioritized second while emergencies are handled. Then what could be day to day normal becomes an emergency while your staff

plays catch up. There is little opportunity to just be. No time to focus on process improvement. You have to bark out orders and hope that things get done. Your staff never has the opportunity to prioritize for themselves. The emergencies dictate the timing of your work.

What it feels like: Stressful and frustrating! An occasional adrenaline rush can be good but if you are running like that all the time, you and your staff are moving towards burn out. You lose efficiency when you are constantly tugged from one task to another. The prior task is forgotten, or it has to be re-done. You waste time getting re-acclimated. Your rock stars will not want to continue working in that environment; they care too much.

What you can do: Are you an adrenaline junky? Is there something in you that enjoys the chaos? Are you artificially creating this environment to feed your need? If so – stop!! Just make an intentional choice to plan ahead. Determine the tasks that your staff will take care of and delegate them well and on time. You can still create some adrenaline rushes for yourself with your own projects but let them experience some peace!

If it's not you, but your office is this disorganized, then you MUST carve out some time for process improvement. Begin slowly if you must, but start the work. Have your team begin to think of processes that could work better. Then, as a team, prioritize the list. As I have said before, when I help a team with this I usually have them start with a few improvements that would be quick fixes with a big impact. I call this, "Big bang for the buck" improvements. Some quick successes will fire your team up to want to do more.

You do not give clear directions: Either you are not organized enough yourself to think clearly about what needs to be done, or you are afraid for some reason. By minimizing your requests or using tentative language, you feel like you are cushioning the blow. Maybe you want your staff to like you. You are afraid of seeming like a tyrant. If this is your fear, trust me, you are probably far from it.

What it looks like: You give out what you think are clear directions but your staff doesn't complete the task. You are not giving any clear call to action. You minimize your delegation with tentative directions like, "When you get to it", or "If you get a chance, can you", or "I was kind of thinking", or "What do you think about", or "Do you think you could". Okay, you get the picture. None of these statements communicates a sense of urgency. If you are telling them to do it when they get the chance, they may never actually get the chance. If you are asking their opinion it sounds like they have the option to do it or not, no big deal.

What it feels like: Frustration and confusion. You are frustrated because it feels like your staff is not listening and never gets anything done. They are confused about what they should actually be doing, "Did he mean that we should start using that form now or are we supposed to wait until he tells us to?"

What you can do: If organization or clear thought is your issue, own it and get help from a staff member who is gifted in that area. Delegate more through your office manager, for example. Meet with him or her to communicate what you want done and talk through the steps to getting there. Pass that Olympic Torch to this champion and let them run with it to your team.

If tentative language is your issue, just be very conscious of your word choices. Drop verbiage that waters down your message. You will notice instantly where you are doing it and should be able to easily switch to more powerful, action-provoking phrases. Also, make sure that you are communicating those deadlines and communication schedules. A deadline alone can create a call to action.

A simple suggestion, but I find with my clients that sometimes if they practice saying what they want in places like their car or at home getting ready for the day or at least think about how they would say it, it is easier to say them when the time actually comes.

You are a Tyrant: Maybe you are overbearing and mean. Perhaps you've been barking orders at your staff and then getting openly angry with them when a task is not done to your specifications. Maybe you have good days and bad. On the bad days, you are using your staff like human punching bags, hitting them with your words. Delegation under these circumstances will be very difficult because your staff members are afraid to take action. They are all trying to hide behind one another. No one wants to be the obvious culprit of the next great offense.

What it looks like: Most of the energy in your clinic is directed at avoiding your wrath. Getting tasks done is secondary. Your patients are secondary. Everyone is walking on eggshells just trying to avoid being the next target. No one wants to stick his or her neck out or take initiative on anything. No one will speak up. That's just like sticking a bullseye on your head.

Your attempts at problem solving will all be met with finger pointing. The energy will be focused on avoiding the wrath and not fixing the problem. Issues will not be resolved. There is little opportunity for good communication as everyone engages in duck and cover or must match your anger in an attempt to be heard.

What it feels like: Your clinic is filled with negative energy, fear, anxiety and anger. At times, some employees may speak back to you but it will not be in an assertive manner. Some will match your anger in an attempt to be heard. Your patients are feeling it. Some are communicating with their feet.

Honestly, if you are acting like a tyrant, the good staff members will not want to work with you for long. Or they will try their hardest and end up with ulcers.

What you can do: Get your anger under control. If you need the assistance of a coach or counselor, do it! If you think reading a book will work, do that. You cannot fire you. You could have the best team in the world but still have negative energy in your facility. You must be your best self to do your important work. You are not being a good steward of your gifts if you are spewing anger. Period.

Nothing your staff members are doing justifies your behavior. Sorry! Maybe you have the worst staff members in the world. Maybe they cannot do the jobs you have hired them to do. The answer is not to yell like a baby. The answer is to take the methodical steps spelled out in this book to get the right staff in and then let them do their jobs.

Catapult Task: Improve Delegation

I have identified these barriers to delegation:

My delegation style has this impact on my clinic:

I have identified these areas where I could delegate better:

I commit to these actions to improve my delegation:

∽∾

Establish Individual Staff Goals

Your employees are on fire with passion and know your mission and vision. You must put strategies in place to ensure that their initiatives are focused on moving you powerfully towards your mission.

Ala Gino Wickman from his book, *Traction,* suggests that you and your business should have a one year plan and 90 day rocks, or outcomes you will create that are measurable. You will not be doing all of the work to help your business achieve the 90 days rocks. Your employees will be assisting. Each quarter, your employees should have new rocks to work on in addition to their every day work. So there are maintenance tasks and move-forward tasks. If your employees' move-forward tasks are aligned with your business mission you will make great progress! You are utilizing them but also allowing them to be a part of the process which provides them with more opportunity to participate and feel ownership in your mission.

Of course, you will also want to include your employees in the planning process. You can use the form below to brainstorm before your meeting and then share it with your team. They may want to renegotiate some of the items. You can allow for that, but you want to make sure your employees are being challenged. Do not allow any cop-outs.

Here is an example:

My Rocks	Related Tasks to Delegate (Team Rocks)	Staff
Incorporate new sample equipment 1 into care plan menu of options	1. Add to patient forms 2. Document procedures 3. Train all PTs on proper use 4. Research & create insurance billing process	1. Front Desk Sue 2. Head PT 3. Head PT 4. Office Manager

Performance Management Process

One of the best tools for assuring that you are communicating expectations to your individual team members and holding them accountable is to engage in a good performance management process. The main difference between performance review and performance management is that the latter involves ongoing communication and goal setting while performance review is generally comprised of just one conversation at the end of the year to "review" what happened the previous year. And, at that point, it's too late to do anything about it. You have potentially traversed 12 months of performance that was less than adequate and the score at the end of the year comes as a complete surprise.

A good performance management system will allow the employee to:

- Learn about his/her own strengths and weaknesses.
- Create new goals and objectives.
- Be an active participant in the evaluation process.
- Create and adult level relationship with the supervisor.
- Work teams may be restructured for maximum efficiency.
- Renew his/her interest in being a part of the organization now and in the future.
- Identify training needs.
- Discuss quality of work.
- Feel that they are taken seriously as individuals and that the supervisor is truly concerned about their needs and goals.

Performance management is an ongoing, continual process of communication. You have scheduled communication activities happening at least once per quarter. It provides a structure for planning and goal setting for individuals and should also include a team component.

The Basics of Performance Management

Let's cover some of the basic terminology of a performance

management process. We need to make distinctions between tasks and behaviors that are requirements of the job and initiatives that go above and beyond.

Performance Standard: the minimum acceptable quality, timeliness and productivity required for the job. It is the baseline by which performance will be measured. Any performance standard should address the following:

- How Well: quality of work
- How Much: quantity of work
- By When: deadlines & dates
- In What Way: procedures, behavioral guidelines

The easiest way to develop performance standards for each job is to begin with the job description. I am hoping that you either had them done already or completed them during the job description catapult task. Each major item from your job description should be referenced in the job's performance management form. Just tweak the requirement to incorporate the additional information of how much, by when, to what degree of accuracy, etc.

Here is a very simple example:

> **Job Description Statement:** Responsible for all billing functions.

> **Performance Standard:** Completes all billing tasks by the 15th of each month with 100% accuracy.

Performance Goal: A new initiative or improvement target that represents a change in expectations but is required by a specified deadline. An example might be asking an employee to research phone systems for the office and make a recommendation by the end of the third quarter. This is also a great place to document the individual employee goals that we discussed above. Only, in this instance, employees will be scored on how well they accomplished them.

Performance Objective: A new and voluntary effort above and beyond essential expectations. Perhaps you have an employee who would like to learn more about patient retention. They may ask for the opportunity to learn about, develop and implement some new patient retention strategies for your office. It is not a requirement, but certainly shows the enthusiasm of an employee. The performance management process gives you the chance to document the request as well as measure and acknowledge success.

Questions to Ask When Completing a Performance Appraisal: Similar to many other sections here, your performance is evaluated first! If employees did not meet the minimum performance standards is there an opportunity for you to learn and improve your leadership style?

- What results did I expect?
- Were these expectations clearly communicated to the employee?
- What contributions should this employee be making?
- Is this employee working near his/her potential?
- What are this employee's strengths?
- What training or other support does he/she need?
- Have I initiated a PIP or other steps towards excellence?
- Have I responded to this employee's requests for resources

or time needed to be successful?

- How has my performance helped or hindered this employee?

Performance Documentation: is an important part of documenting employee performance. I recommend including specific examples of performance that substantiates any score falling either above or below the standard. You will also use this criteria when conducting any discipline that relates to deficient performance. All performance documentation should be:

- Factual: Events & Observations
- Include Date(s)
- Consistently applied for all employees

Performance Documentation is NOT:

- Opinions
- Assumptions, speculations, conclusions
- Personal descriptions
- Data about employee's personal life
- Promises
- WHY you think it happened

In other words, it is not your job to diagnose why the performance was deficient. This gets into too many subjective areas and also may create a scenario where you are getting pulled in to the "Life is Hard" sympathy card. Steer clear of that by committing to sticking to facts only.

The Performance Management Form:

I usually recommend using a scored section that includes the core values of the organization and also the specific tasks of the job. The core values would be the same for every job while the tasks section would be specific to each position and will include the standard of performance required to meet expectations.

An example from the core values might be customer service. If you have a core value to provide wow patient care, you would have a line on the performance management form dedicated to that one trait. Each employee would then be scored on his or her contribution to that core value within your clinic.

I always endorse a very simple form that totals the score. You can also give varying weight to each section. You need a column for the trait they are being scored on, a short column for the score, one for the weight and a wider column for any notes regarding the specific scored item.

Individual Performance Ratings

I always recommend using a scoring system with just 3 levels. There is no need to complicate things! Adding more levels makes it too difficult to differentiate. After all, if you have a rock star employee who goes above and beyond often, at what point do they move from a 4 star rock star to a 5? What level of performance would it take? It's difficult to define. And you want to keep your system as objective as possible. So, just keep it simple.

1 = Does Not Meet Expectations

2 = Successfully Meets Expectations

3 = Consistently Exceeds Expectations

Annual Meeting

The annual meeting is a great time for you to practice your leadership in service skills. Remember, this is the art of looking at what you could have done better first. As you prepare for the meeting you should take a look at the role you played in each employee's performance. Did you communicate expectations well, hold people accountable, work to create a great culture, provide the resources and time required to be successful? It all begins with you.

The annual meeting will include a look back at the previous year. You and your employee should talk about what went well and what could have gone better with an opportunity to identify goals for growth. You will want to focus on excellence rather than excuses. Barriers are seen as challenges to overcome rather than excuses to lower the bar.

As you communicate the expectations for the next year do not miss out on this valuable opportunity to tie everything to your bigger mission. Make sure to speak but leave plenty of time to listen and problem solve. Over time the annual performance management meeting should come to be a time that your employees look forward to. It should be a great bonding time.

Individual Goals

Take the time to develop some individual goals. Again, these should be initiatives that go beyond what is routinely required of the position. Encourage your team to work new muscles by taking on stretch goals that require them to learn new skills or practice new techniques.

Start by talking about how your team member can impact the company. Maybe they have seen some areas that could use improvement and are happy to take them on as a project. Are there any educational goals that would help your clinic? What about some personal goals? You don't want to go too deep into the personal realm but you can allow the employee to document a few general personal goals on their annual performance management form. Creating healthier personal lives will enable employees to be more productive at work too. Maybe they want to commit to more exercise or take a stress management class.

Team Goals

You definitely do not want to create an environment where it is every man or woman for himself so you should also include some team goals in your performance management system. Keep the concept of working together front and center in everyone's mind and provide the opportunity for everyone to rally around a common mission that, ultimately, moves you closer to yours. I usually recommend allocating twenty percent of the overall performance summary score to the team portion.

Coming up with good team goals can be a bit tricky, though. You want to make sure that everyone has a say. Creating the goals is not something that you want achieved behind closed doors. Make sure to incorporate it into some of your team meetings. Assure that they are goals that everyone can participate in because the entire team will get the same rating and use quantifiable/strategic goals that are tied to your mission. Some examples would be goals that focus around your patient statistics or satisfaction scores. Or, create some targets for collecting a specific number of high quality, positive testimonials on your website.

Interim Progress Discussion

You should have interim progress discussions two times per year, at least initially to encourage ongoing communication. This discussion is meant to be informal. The goal is to give you a scheduled opportunity to sit down with your employees individually to discuss how things are going, what support they need, any additional resources they require, and what is going well. I recommend that you use a uniform set of questions as a guideline for getting started but that the conversation be very free form. There is a sample list of questions in the appendix at the end of the book. The employee should be responsible for completing the questionnaire prior to the meeting and should be in charge of determining the flow of topics. Overtime, perhaps performance communication will become a standard part of your operating procedure and you will no longer need two formal meetings. They are very important, however, so do not eliminate them while they are still playing an important part in the flow of communication in your business.

Performance Improvement Plan:

A Performance Improvement Plan (PIP) is a written agreement between an employee and his/her manager that identifies opportunities for growth and the expectations for improvement over a specified period. I like to think of a PIP as a positive correction. You are documenting changes and learning what an employee must do to meet the standards of his or her job. You are also making a promise to them to help them improve. So, you are making a commitment to invest in their growth.

In the PIP, you or the supervisor will spell out specifically what behaviors or skills need to be modified, any steps required to get there, and deadlines. The PIP will also identify specific training activities that an employee must complete. The employee and supervisor will schedule and document some routine meetings to assess progress. The number of meetings and intervals will be determined by the extent of change required and the duration of the training.

It is also important to give the employee full accountability for keeping the scheduled meetings, requesting additional help, etc. The employee is responsible for reporting any circumstances that impedes his/her ability to successfully complete the guidelines of the PIP. You must communicate all of this succinctly.

The PIP can be done in conjunction with your discipline process if appropriate but can also stand alone. Or it can be used as a way of documenting necessary change identified during an annual performance management communication meeting.

If used in conjunction with discipline, the PIP does not affect the progression of the disciplinary process. It is not considered to be a step in that process. However, failure to adhere to the agreement spelled out in the PIP can result in disciplinary action.

You can find a sample Performance Improvement Plan in the Appendix.

Catapult Task: Communicating Clear Expectations

We have fallen short in communicating clear expectations in these ways:

I commit to utilizing individual goals in this way:

We have these issues with our current performance management system:

We will make these changes in our performance management process:

I see the need for a PIP in these areas:

I commit to following through with PIPs based on my KSA evaluations:

❧

Section 3:
Convene Your Remarkable Team

Snowflakes are one of nature's most fragile things,
but just look at what they can do when they stick together.
-Vesta Kelly

By this point, you have given your individual team members plenty of opportunities to exhibit their excitement and passion about your mission. You should have a clear understanding of where each employee excels and struggles in terms of their knowledge, skills and abilities. Hopefully, you have implemented some strategies to address shortfalls among solid team members and have been providing plenty of opportunities for them to participate with you on your journey to mission. Perhaps you have initiated a Performance Improvement Plan.

My guess is that some things still are not quite right. You are still being blindsided here and there. Because the tough work is not quite done.

When I vacuum in my family room, I use the same outlet because I am a creature of habit, like most, and because it's in a good location. I like to listen to my iPod and really get down to the business of cleaning. I am efficient and task-oriented. The problem is that often, when I use this plug, just when I'm really getting into the groove of vacuuming suddenly the circuit breaker trips. It stops me dead in my tracks. What the heck happened?!? I am thrown for a loop. I have to go downstairs, trip the switch and plug the vacuum into another outlet (only to forget again the next time!). I have to refocus – get back in my groove.

How often does this happen in your practice? You get cranking along, have good patient flow going, feels like the staff is gelling, then – Boom – there's drama, hurt feelings, gossip, dropped processes, excuses, bad energy, ill feelings, resentments, poor communication – and your flow is all gone. You have to reposition; you lose momentum.

If you allow employees to break your flow, you are losing efficiency, failing your patients and frustrating your rock stars. The negative energy in your clinic creates collateral damage. A conflict between two employees rarely affects just the two.

Think about the last time this happened in your practice. What was the issue? What was the result? Try to think of all of the consequences, rather than just the most obvious. What was your response? Did you engage in duck and cover? Did you try to help fix it or did you encourage your staff to work it out? Did you work towards creating a culture where drama would not be tolerated or did you fuel the fire by putting extra focus and energy there, giving the drama seekers their fix of time and attention.

The goal is to have a practice with no short circuits, no surprise attacks. We will cover the basic steps for removing the short circuits and creating a remarkable team so that you and your patients can experience a clear path of positive energy.

ഗൗ

Defined Consequences:
The Tools of Great Accountability

While we are free to choose our actions, we are not free to choose the consequences of our actions. ~ Stephen R. Covey

A key ingredient in the formula for creating a remarkable team is a culture of accountability. To create accountability you must have clear expectations and consistent, objective consequences. Consistent accountability requires having an HR Policy Manual and sticking to it. It helps you objectively follow through with progressive discipline when necessary.

This does not mean taking your discipline to the extreme and creating a culture of fear; you are just looking for opportunities to assert yourself. Give clear directions utilizing your great delegation techniques, provide your staff with the tools needed, and if they fail to follow your instructions follow through as promised with all staff. Even your rock stars might falter here and there. If you allow them more leeway, it will cause drama as other staff members begin to feel resentment. And your rock stars can begin to think they are above the law. You do not want that.

Great delegation requires good, consistent and defined consequences. While I believe most people want to do a good job, there are times when employees fall short. Some employees need a little external motivation to achieve excellence. Still others just cannot seem to get it at all. For these circumstances, there must be consequences spelled out up front. Not each time you delegate, of course, but as tools in your tool belt as you run your day-to-day operation.

Similar to raising kids, you need to set the consequences up front and then follow through consistently where necessary.

With the right staff, you will need to use these tools only occasionally. However, if this book is showing you a tough transition is required, you or your designate may be using these tools quite a bit initially.

The first and most important tool in your tool belt is the Progressive Discipline Process.

Utilize a Progressive Discipline Process

A good discipline process is no more than detailing the consequences of inappropriate behavior, in writing. It is titled progressive discipline because there are a series of steps outlined that get progressively worse.

The key to the process is to follow it. It does you no good to have a discipline process sitting in a binder getting dusty. Moreover, you must follow it consistently. You cannot play favorites. If you have family members on your team, they cannot be exempt. That sets a very poor example and will lead to all kinds of drama.

I have used this example before but it really is no different from spelling out the rules of the home for your child, communicating the consequences of breaking those rules and then following through on your word. Your employees are like your kids. If you have stated rules but do not follow through with the consequences, those rules will not dictate behavior.

To me, the discipline process is something that you have in your tool belt that you should need only seldom. Once your staff realizes you will follow through with consequences, they will follow the rules. They do not want to be written up or lose their jobs. If you implement a discipline process and they do not care, you do not have the right staff. No problem. Just take them through the process and get them exited out. Win – Win either way!

Trust me; your rock stars love a great discipline process. It will keep the other staff in line. If someone is complaining about it, they are already trying to find a way around your rules.

Consult with a professional if you need assistance. This may not be your forte and that is okay. Others love this part office management. Better to get the right tools in place than to let something simple stop you.

Recommendations for a Progressive Discipline Process

Some infractions are more serious than others. In general, violations that are more serious will result in more serious disciplinary action. Based on that premise, I recommend dividing the work rules in to two groups:

- **Group I Violations:** are less serious in nature. Violations will result in the progressive disciplinary steps described in this section.

- **Group II Violations:** are considered very serious and any violation will generally result in immediate discharge or at least some time off without pay.

The Four Levels of Disciplinary Action

Corrective Action Notice

A Corrective Action Notice should be issued for a first violation of a Group I work rule violation. At this step, the supervisor should tell the employee exactly what offense has been committed and outline the proper action that must be followed to correct the situation. The employee is encouraged to explain his/her actions. The employee should also be asked to sign a copy of the Corrective Action Notice to indicate that he/she has read it. The notice becomes a part of the employee's file. If there is no further discipline within a 12-month time period, the notice will no longer be considered for the purpose of progressive discipline.

First-Level Written Warning

A first –level written warning is given if the employee has committed what could be considered a Group I rule violation and has previously received a Corrective Action Notice for a Group I rule violation within the last 12 months. A written warning details the offense and the policy involved. If the employee disagrees with any of the facts, he/she should have the opportunity to add a statement to the record. Again, the employee should be asked to sign a copy of the warning to indicate that he/ she has read it. This warning becomes a part of the employee's record. If no further offenses occur within a 12-month time period, the warning will no longer be considered for the purpose of progressive discipline.

Second-Level Written Warning

A second-level written warning should be issued for any violation if an employee has received a first-level written warning within the last 12 months. Or, if the employee has engaged in activity that falls under a Group II violation. At this level, a one- to-five day suspension without pay may accompany a written warning for violations other than absenteeism or tardiness.

Third-Level Written Warning

Receiving a third-level written warning for any violation within a 12-month period should be cause for discharge if the employee has two active written warnings. You may also go straight to a Third-Level Written Warning if the offense is especially egregious. In either case, the third written warning should result in termination of employment.

You will also find a sample Progressive Discipline Form in the Appendix.

Catapult Task: Discipline Process

I commit to creating and rolling out a discipline process for my organization or using the one we have:

I commit to following up with discipline when it is appropriate:

⚮

Address People Problems

Now let's cover some additional strategies to help you remain consistent and fair as you convene your remarkable team. You want to minimize the opportunity for drama and encourage excellence. A good rule to lead by is that you can demand no more from your staff than you do from your lowest performing employee.

Stop and think about that for a minute. Picture your most difficult staff member. How much drama do they create? How many excuses do they give? How ineffective are they?

Now, picture every staff member functioning at that same level. Every time I do this presentation, I get a laugh during this part. It is almost universal. At least one employee always easily comes to mind.

Really, visualize:

- What would your practice be like?
- How would it function?
- What would it feel like for your patients?
- Would your billing get done?
- Would your phone get answered?
- Would patient charts be up to date and filed?
- What kind of energy would you have in your practice?

Your other employees are accommodating the performance you allow from that individual. They are working harder, picking up slack, dealing with unnecessary drama, trying to protect your patients, and trying to protect you. And they are building up resentment.

If it is really bad, your great employees will get burned out and decide to go elsewhere. You will be left with that poor performer who has fewer options. If this is your circumstance, those satisfied with the drama and chaos are happy because they are the cause and it is working for them!

You cannot tolerate anything less than excellence! You have important work to do and you need top-notch employees to help you get there. Your staff is an extension of you! How many patients have you lost due to rude treatment from your staff? Or how many are barely tolerating it because they feel such loyalty to you. This is not what you want for your patients!

You want your patients to have an excellent experience with you from start to finish. Fill your practice with the right kind of employees and processes and they will.

You can not create a remarkable team with dead weight. Most health professionals who hire me have at least one employee who is not a right fit. We start by transforming the leadership style, making sure that everyone has the opportunity to be successful, and, inevitably, there is at least one person who thinks they will be able to continue to behave the way they have all along. They are usually the victim person or the "Life is Hard" sympathy card employee. They often claim their employers are "just out to get me." They use all kinds of defense mechanisms to stay exactly as they are and try to change the world around them to meet their needs.

If you have one or more of these people in your clinic, they do have to go. Your other staff members will grow, learn, transform and will work hard to establish a new culture and improved energy. This employee will do everything in his or her power to sabotage those efforts. There is always collateral damage when you have a staff member who does not wish to do the right thing. If they are unproductive, they are not just stealing work hours. They are creating resentment in your other staff members who are picking up the slack.

This is where that right mindset you worked on earlier needs to kick in. You were born with a heart to serve but must work around that to lead well here. It is a privilege to work for you, not an entitlement or a right. If they have financial needs, it is not up to you to give them the means to fulfill their obligations. It is up to them. A self-actualized person who needs money will make the right choices to keep their job. They will not look to others to create an environment that suits them to keep a position. There is no guilt here. Each employee has free will. If you are doing everything in your power to allow them the opportunity to be successful and they are still choosing to fail, it is their choice, their doing. Release them out into the world to find a work environment that better fits who they want to be on the job. They will be happier in the end and so will your team.

There are two basic termination types that may be appropriate at this point. They are:

Performance based termination: the employee just does not have the knowledge, skills or abilities to be successful. You have done the analysis and do not see a way for them to get to where you need them. You also have no alternative position where their skill sets could be better utilized. They are not a fit.

> **Form:** I recommend initiating a Performance Improvement Plan in this instance. Use the form to document specifically what skill sets or knowledge is lacking and outline a plan for the employee to gain the knowledge or skills that they need. You also may want to share with them the evaluation you did of their position.

> **Process:** Schedule a private meeting to go over the plan with him or her in detail. Provide an opportunity for your employee to give you feedback. Maybe they have some untapped skills of which you are not aware. Speak frankly with them about your concerns and communicate with clarity about where you need them to be. If they initially feel like the plan you outline is feasible, allow them some time to try. Maintain the regularly scheduled meetings that you have outlined on the PIP form to monitor whether or not

they are making progress. Continue to have frank open and honest discussions. Be sure to document all of your conversations and have the employee sign off on your notes after each meeting.

Outcome: Maybe you get to experience the win-win of having the employee rise to the occasion and surpass your expectations. You will get to reap the benefit of salvaging an existing employee. Worse case scenario is that after some time you determine that your initial feelings were correct and they need to go. If the employee handled himself or herself professionally, offer to provide a letter of recommendation and let them leave on good terms.

Behavior based termination: the employee is exhibiting a negative attitude, balking at change, engaging in sabotage, has attendance issues, is defensive or argumentative. You have communicated the expectations of continued employment clearly but he or she is continuing to make poor choices.

Form: In this instance, you will use the Progressive Discipline Form.

Process: Follow the progressive discipline process as outlined in the prior chapter. Begin with a Corrective Action Notice (it is all on the same form). This is the equivalent of a verbal warning but you will have written documentation. Complete the form accurately providing specific examples and spell out exactly what behaviors the employee must change. Schedule a private meeting to communicate the issues and your expectations. You can have a second person there as support or as a witness if you feel it is necessary. Ideally, this would be an office manager or a trusted advisor with human resource experience.

As you begin the meeting, ask the employee to listen until you are finished and tell them that they will have a chance to speak after you are through. Continue to emphasize that you want them to be successful and that you hope they will make the right choices. This communicates to them that there is no one else to blame and will help to reinforce the concept for you as well, in case you are feeling guilty unnecessarily.

When you are through have the employee sign the form. They may add a few written comments if they wish.

Do not allow the employee to exhibit anger or get defensive. Keep the entire meeting short and sweet. Stick to the point. If he or she attempts to highjack the meeting do not allow it. They may use deflection techniques that take the focus off themselves. For instance, they may try to tell you about other employees in the clinic and their offenses. Just keep bringing the conversation back to them with simple phrases like, "We are not meeting about them. We are here to discuss your performance." Or you might say, "That is not your concern. I would like you to focus on you right now." If they continue to get off topic or escalate their anger end the meeting with a warning that they must behave professionally or there will be additional disciplinary action immediately.

Needless to say, their reaction during the meeting usually gives you a good indication of whether they are going to make the necessary changes to be successful going forward. Ideally, the discipline is a wakeup call. They will see that you are serious and will choose to alter their behavior to keep their job. If not, just keep walking them through the discipline process until they are out the door.

Outcome: Either you get a transformed employee who realizes that they no longer have the power to dictate the culture of your organization or that employee is no longer there wreaking havoc. Either way you win! Additionally, other employees will see that you are serious and will be less apt to test the waters.

Documentation in either case is important. It provides a good tool for communicating clear expectations but you have also created a paper trail that evidences your attempts at helping your employee be successful. Often my clients fear the repercussions of a lawsuit. Those fears are not without merit. I always say that you can not stop someone from filing suit you can only prepare yourself in case it happens. Frivolous lawsuits do happen after a termination but most former employees do not take that action. So, just make sure that you have documentation. Even unemployment claims can be thwarted with good documentation. Do not let fear stop you here. What cost are you incurring by keeping poor performers on board? Remember, it is not just the lost productivity from these individuals but also the collateral damage they create within your business and amongst the other staff.

Remember, you can always call on a trusted advisor with human resource expertise if you feel uncertain.

Catapult Task: **Addressing Your People Problems**

I concede that these employees do not fit with the remarkable team that I am creating:

My patients, business and team are suffering these consequences as a result:

I commit to the following actions to address these shortfalls to provide these employees with an opportunity to be successful if they make the right choices:

✐✐

Encourage Energy Boosting Behavior

The world belongs to the energetic ~ Ralph Waldo Emerson

Encourage your individual employees to choose high energy. I define energy boosters as people who are positive and upbeat. They leave their life issues at the door and arrive at work ready to focus on your patients. They have a can do attitude and are great team players. Energy busters, on the other hand, have sour moods. They can be whiney and self-centered. They bring their life issues to work and seek support from co-workers for each new self-inflicted challenge they face.

In the earlier chapters on energy and mood we went into great detail about intentionally choosing to protect your energy. I won't go through it again. I will just encourage you to share those concepts with your team.

In my team building workshops, I challenge staff members to make an intentional choice to be energy boosters, not busters. I encourage you to do the same with your team. It does take effort to hit it every day, but you can do it and they can too. Share with them the strategies from the protecting your energy section of the book.

Here is a list of qualities to help you determine which of your team are energy boosters and which are energy busters.

Energy Busters Exhibit:

- Negative Thinking
- Victim Mentality
- Poor or Aggressive Communication
- Gossip
- Backstabbing
- Focus On Self or Personal Problems
- Frustration
- Sense of Entitlement

Energy Boosters Exhibit:

- Gratitude
- Focus on Helping Others
- Positive Thinking
- Assertive Communication
- Giving
- Happiness
- Teamwork
- Problem Solving

⌒⌒

Create a Laser Focus on Your Vision and Your Patients

The more you lose yourself in something bigger than yourself, the more energy you will have.
-Norman Vincent Peale

A remarkable team fully aligned with a mission and an outward focus on patients does not have time to gossip, worry about who is doing what, or who is on their cell phone. They will be working like a well-oiled machine, focused and fully engaged on their purpose. Do all you can to focus your team. Make a game of reaching hefty goals weekly or monthly; constantly remind them of the importance of their work. Each member of your staff needs to know the value of their position and its role in your clinic.

Implement "Drop Everything Service". No task is more important than meeting your patient needs.

Develop a vision of the ultimate patient experience in the clinic. What should it feel like for a patient when they walk in the clinic? What kind of energy, service and care should they receive? Each employee needs to know how he or she can help enhance the patient experience. Make a game out of it. Keep the focus on the ever-increasing goal of improving your patient experience.

Catapult Task: Ultimate Patient Experience

Work with your team to create a vision for the ultimate patient experience:

Define what needs to change to create it:

Assign duties to team members or allow them to volunteer to help make it a reality:

✧

Encourage Team Communication

The problem with communication is the illusion that is has occurred. – George Bernard Shaw

Even people in healthy relationships have disagreements periodically. It is a normal part of human interaction. Seeing some healthy conflict means that your team is engaged in your business and feels confident enough to speak up. This is a good thing. A silent meeting is the sign of an unhealthy team. Employees are afraid to speak up, are harboring resentments with each other, do not trust one another or just do not care enough to exert the effort to voice an opinion.

Encourage healthy discussions and debates. You want everyone to have a voice. You just never know where that next great idea might come from.

And when there is a conflict, encourage your team members to work out their differences themselves wherever possible. If a grievance is worth spending any time on it should be productive time used to improve the situation rather than just for gossiping and complaining.

Pull yourself and everyone else out of the mediator role. Think how much time that wastes! Spending time on petty disagreements and hurts just sends that message that it's okay to engage in them. You can end up with employees pitting themselves against one another or vying for your attention with protests.

If you have been at the center of many of the team conflicts you will need to communicate the new expectation and then stand your ground. Their first instincts will probably be to involve you initially. Transition yourself and/or your office manager out by saying something like, "I understand that you are feeling frustrated. I need you to go have a conversation directly with X. If you need additional assistance afterward let me know."

You or your office manager may need to act as mediator initially but all communication happens with interested parties in the room. No longer tolerate he said she said. And those embroiled in the conflict must address each other in the meeting not you.

Create a gossip-free zone where communication about an issue must be with the person(s) involved, period.

Provide assertive communication training if necessary. That is the gold standard for communication.

Here is a simple little formula you can teach your team to use when they have a disagreement. It can be modified for any situation and, as you can see, the responsibility of finding a solution rests with the person bringing up the issue.

1. When you:_____

2. I feel:_____

3. Can you please:_____

⮜⧽⧼⮞

Create Team Commitments

Individual commitment to a group effort –
that is what makes a team work, a company work,
a society work. ~ Vince Lombardi

When we are in positive relationships, we have positive thoughts and feelings about each other. We fill in the blanks of the unknown with positive assumptions. We give each other the benefit of the doubt. If someone does not complete a task we say, "They must have had a very busy day," or, "It must have slipped her mind."

When relationships begin to go south, however, we start to assume the worst. I often refer to this phenomenon as the downward spiral. If someone does not complete a task, we decide that they are lazy or trying to dump work.

Often these assumptions become truth to us and we are not even aware that we are doing it! Our "truths' alter the way we relate to the people in our lives. And the way we relate to others contributes to the design of the relationship.

Think about your own relationships for a minute. I am sure that you have some people in your life (or perhaps a bit removed from your life) who you believe to be very self-centered. Now stop to think about how the view of them shapes the way you communicate with that person. Maybe they are the kind who seem to do nothing but complain. Their life is way worse than anyone else's. Do you try to avoid them as a result or do you end up getting in a competition of my life is worse than yours?

Now consider the overbearing person who has an opinion about everything. Think about how you censor yourself around them. Do you end up withholding information as a result? That relationship is formed differently as a result of your censoring. They may experience you as closed off. I am not saying it is not warranted. This section isn't about evaluating whether you are right or wrong. I just want you to gain some awareness about how many of your assumptions or evaluations of others do impact the way you relate to them.

Now think about a trusted advisor you utilize, the person who avoids judgment, who shares advice without attachment and holds shared information as strictly confidential. How do you relate to this person? How do your conversations compare with the person who always has an opinion and speaks too much?

While we are all entitled to our opinions about others, the exercise is about helping them realize and know that their opinions are not necessarily fact.

Encourage your team to do some reality-checking around the assumptions they are making about each other. If your team is still in a good upward spiral this will be an easy exercise. If, however, they have slipped and no longer have faith or trust in each other you will have your work cut out for you.

If they trust each other enough to be open, have a good discussion during one of your team meetings. Mediate some conversations between people and departments. You may want to enlist the help of a professional coach if the team dynamic has really deteriorated, though. You don't want the exercise to morph into a big complaint session that ends with people's feelings hurt and even great divides between team members.

Once they get through the muck, have your team make commitments to each other about what they will think and how they will relate to each other now and in the future. If you are behind the eight ball on this one and have some clean up work to do continue to encourage what may be a longer journey to trust and open communication.

Here are some examples of commitments that some of my clients' teams have established:

- We will assume our co-workers are doing their best.
- We commit to avoiding gossip.
- We commit to resolving our conflicts with good communication.
- We commit to treating each other with respect.
- We will assume that our team mates want to do a good job.

❧ ❦

Utilize Process Improvement

We covered this topic before but it warrants another pass under this topic. Very often, when processes are not functioning well, people will assume that the lost productivity or frustration that they are experiencing is the fault of a team member. This is particularly true when you have a team that is already in a downward relationship spiral. It just makes things worse. Worse relationships mean more drama. So, if you did not read it well, go back to the process improvement section and brush up.

Require your team members to offer at least one solution to every problem they point out.

They have no ownership in the problems or the solutions if they are allowed to just complain. Implement the Gripe and Grumble Form if you have not already. The easiest part of creating change is pointing out a problem. That is just the starting point. Hold them to a higher standard

> *A business' success is often in direct*
> *proportion to its ability to fix issues.*

❦

Generate "Right-Hiring"

Do not hire a man who does your work for money,
but him who does it for love of it. ~ Henry David Thoreau

By this time, you have done quite a bit of analysis about how your staff is functioning. There may be some staff members not making the grade. Maybe you are thinking, "Well, I'm not going to get anything better. The last time I hired someone this is what I got. At least my current employee is trained. They know my practice inside and out. I don't want to start from scratch!"

If this is your thinking, you are selling yourself short, way short! You are justifying and letting your fear of the unknown stop you in your tracks. You fear the conversation. You fear unemployment paperwork arriving. You fear running the clinic without them while you find the replacement. You fear making the same hiring mistake again and getting the same or someone worse.

I get it! It is scary but I am here to tell you that it can be done. You can find a great employee and we are going to cover some of the basics now.

Generating right-hiring , in a nutshell, is all about finding the RIGHT person not just A person. You don't want to settle for just a warm body. You want someone exceptional. And the word generate is used intentionally. It takes action, the right kind of action, to create great hiring. The right person rarely falls spontaneously into your waiting room at the precise moment you need him or her. Finding the right person requires precise action, objectivity and sometimes patience.

How far did you cast your net the last time you were hiring? Did your entire open position posting process consist of telling a few patients, family members, and friends that you were looking for someone? I have news for you; there are simple ways to cast your net way farther than that!

Does this response sound at all familiar? "Oh, I know someone. She's really nice. She was just fired because her old boss was a jerk. She really needs the money! I'm sure she'd work here! It's right by her house, so it would be perfect!"

Do you want to be convenient? Or do you want to provide a place for someone to stretch their skills and fulfill their life's purpose?

The definition of the right person in this context is one who has the true passion for the work, the heartfelt desire to do it, and the unique abilities that meet your clinic's needs. As I said earlier, we are all born with gifts that we are to use in service to others. Thus, the world is comprised of people with widely varying personalities and talents. The innate gifts and abilities define how we are "wired" and cannot be reconfigured. These are aspects of our being that cannot be taught. That is the reality and it is an important, unwavering concept to understand before beginning any hiring activities.

Regardless of where they will work in your clinic, you are looking for someone who has the passion and desire to help your patients. Someone who has that heart to serve, has empathy when people are in pain or struggling, and who has the ability to work well with others. Additionally, I think that you will want them to have the skills to stay organized, communicate effectively, someone who can learn the processes in your clinic and is willing to constantly look for better ways to do things.

This all sounds too good to be true, right? Well, believe it, or not, finding people with these attributes is possible! And, there is a simple way to determine whether your candidate possesses these qualities during an interview. The key is to use behavioral based interviewing. The premise of this interview technique is that the best predictor of future behavior is past behavior. Someone possessing a real heart to serve will be able to share story after story of specific times they went above and beyond for a customer or patient. Someone who takes initiative will have multiple examples of stepping up and fixing an error or improving a process.

While the ideal candidate will possess the right behaviors and specific skills, I always err on the side of focusing on the behaviors. You can teach someone your billing system or appointment scheduling software but you cannot teach her how to care.

Obviously, some positions are going to require specific education or certifications. You cannot train someone to be a Registered Nurse on the job. But, you can hire an RN with the right heart to heal and teach her your systems. I would choose that person over an RN who knows your system but has a sense of entitlement any day!

In case hiring has felt like a daunting task that you'll avoid at all cost, here are the basics of preparing for and designing a recruiting process that will secure you that awesome employee that you and your practice deserve! If you delegate this task, just share this section.

You may also want to consider utilizing a retained search professional at first. For a comparatively nominal fee they will do all of the upfront work of posting and prescreening. You then have the luxury of seeing just your final top candidates. Moreover, most will include a guarantee. While it is unlikely, if that new employee is not what he or she was billed as, the search is reopened free of charge.

The Interview Process in a Nutshell

A good interview process is about finding a great fit, not just a warm body! It takes planning and an intentional process.

By hiring the wrong person, you add significant costs:

- An ineffective team
- Lost productivity
- Wages spent on time dealing with employee issues
- Employee complaints
- Patient or customer complaints
- Lost patients who communicate with their feet

Becoming a great interviewer just takes some practice. Starting with a good process definitely helps. Here are some of the basic steps of a good solid interview.

Getting Word Out About Your Job

Earlier I talked about going only as far as your clinic waiting room to announce a job opening. You need to cast your net wider! And today it's easier and more cost effective than ever. The first step is to create a good job description.

Create a Job Posting

The job posting should summarize the basic job duties as well as requirements of the job. The goal is to make it short and sweet but also comprehensive. Bullet points work great. People don't have a long attention span on the internet, and that's where you'll be putting this description.

If you completed the job description exercise earlier in the book you are all set. You can start there. Just pick out the key duties. And, for requirements, make sure to include the following:

Required Skills

- Mandatory Skills – Required by State or Federal Regulations
- Require Special Schooling or Training
- Cannot be easily learned on the job

Skills that are Nice to Have

- Skills not mandated by any State or Federal Regulations
- Are transferable from other employers
- Can be trained on the job if necessary

Desired Behaviors/Performance Skills (these are non-negotiable)

- Keep in mind that these may be harder to train than skills!

- Examples include; Customer/Patient Oriented, Takes initiative, Creativity

I also always recommend including the salary. If someone is not willing to work for what you are willing to pay I would rather have them self-select out than waste time reading their resume and doing an initial interview only to find out they are not a true potential candidate.

Post the Job

Once you have it created, post your job opening online so that lots and lots of people can see it, cast your net large! If you want to remain anonymous, don't worry. You don't have to put the name of your company or any identifying information. Some of the online listing sites will anonymize your email for you (keep it hidden). You can also create a free email that gives no identifying information through hotmail.com, gmail.com, yahoo.com or any number of other free email sites.

For posting, I recommend starting with Craigslist.org. It is free for most locations and it is where many people go to look for jobs. Select your geographic location and the job category. Ebay.com also has a classified section now. It is currently free. You can also try the unemployment site for your state. In Michigan it's Michigan Talent Bank. You can subscribe as an employer to post jobs or search resumes.

Social Media Posting Options

If you are a bit more savvy on the internet you may have a Twitter account or Facebook page. Or, perhaps you utilize Linkedin. Social Media sites are another great way to get word out about your job. On Linkedin you can join job groups relevant to the position you are trying to fill. Most allow you to post open positions free of charge. Some even have a designated job board.

On Twitter, post the basics of the job in a short snippet. You only get 140 characters. And include a shortened link to your Craigslist post where they'll get the full detail. To shorten your link, use tinyurl. com.

To gain more traffic to your post include a hash tag with the word job like this #Job. Also include a separate hash tag with the job title or professional category. #Job #RN, for instance.

The hash sign on Twitter is used to denote a keyword or phrase that will become searchable. A well informed Twitter user, and there are many, knows to conduct specific searches on words that include the # sign. So, those highly qualified RN's who are looking for work will be out on Twitter searching for posts that include the words #Job #RN and they will find you!

Screening Resumes

If you are worried about getting too many resumes, it is a valid concern. You will get a lot of resumes for most positions you post. That can be good, lots to choose from. But, that can be bad, lots to choose from! It is time-consuming weeding through sometimes hundreds of resumes. Here are some time-saving tips:

1. Require that they put their resume in the body of their response email. It really does save a lot of time not having to open attachments for every email you receive. It's also safer. Attachments can sometimes contain viruses. Knock on wood, it hasn't happened to me after perusing thousands of emailed resumes, but the risk is always there.

2. Know exactly what you are looking for and immediately screen out resumes that don't have at least the basics. Create an email folder with the title of the position and "no interview". If they don't meet the minimum criteria or are overqualified, close the email back up and move it to this folder right away.

3. If a resume has promise, flag it right away. If it looks really, really good at first glance flag it and move it to an "interview" folder that you've created for the specific position.

4. Once you have accumulated 20 or 30 flagged resumes in your interview folder begin emailing them to schedule quick 15 to 20 minute phone interviews. This will narrow your pool more.

5. Repeat this process until you have a good number of prequalified candidates to interview in person.

Planning the Interview

Once you have screened through resumes and done phone interviews your candidate pool should be narrowed to a manageable number that you will meet face to face for an interview. Ideally, you conduct the interview at your location so that you can conclude with a short tour.

Review the Required Skills

- Mandatory Skills – Required by State or Federal Regulations
- Require Special Schooling or Training
- Cannot be easily taught on the job

Revisit the Skills that are Nice to Have

- Skills not mandated by any State or Federal Regulations
- Are transferable from other employers
- Can be trained on the job if necessary

Review the Desired Behaviors/Performance Skills (these are non-negotiable)

- Keep in mind that these may be harder to train than skills!
- Examples include; Customer/Patient Oriented, Takes initiative, Creativity

Review Resumes Looking for:

- Required Skills/Education
- Gaps in Service
- Significant Achievements
- Experience Related to the Job
- Overall Appearance (spelling, grammar, etc.)

Establish a Good Climate for the Interview

Make sure that you have a good comfortable spot for the interview. I am a firm believer in doing all you can to bring out the best in the candidate. Many people become very stressed during an interview anyway. There is no need to add more fuel to that fire. Make sure that you have privacy and will experience no interruptions. Turn your phone off. Shut the door and alert your co-workers. Plan plenty of time so that you aren't rushed.

Build Rapport with the Candidate

Do not keep your candidate waiting. Plan to start on time. Greet your candidate warmly and then make some small talk as you walk them back to your interview space. Ask if they found you easily, talk about the weather. The topic does not matter much, just keep it light.

Once in the room invite them to be seated and explain how the interview will progress. If you plan to take notes tell them up front. I usually also tell them that I will ask my questions and tell them that they will have time for questions at the end. This does two things: it lets them know what to expect but also sends the message that the interview will be give and take. They will have time for questions and I expect that they are just as interested in gathering more information about the company as I am about gathering information about them.

Gather Information about the Candidate

- **Get clarification on any relevant skills, experience or education:** Go through the resume and dive into the skills, experience and education required and/or nice to have for the job.

- **Ask about any gaps in service:** If you see some large gaps in their employment ask casually but do not probe about anything personal or that is not relevant to the job. For instance, if they say they took time off to stay home with kids, acknowledge it and move on. Do not ask how old they are or whether they plan to have more. We will cover illegal questions in more detail later in this chapter.

- **Use Prepared Behavioral Questions, as discussed below. Include at least one question for each identified performance skill.** You will find a list of example behavioral based interviewing questions in the Appendix.

- Behavioral based question assumes that past behavior is the best predictor of future behavior. You are asking for specific examples of what the candidate has done – NOT what they WOULD do. Stay away from "would" questions.

  Here is an example of a question you would ask to determine whether the candidate is customer service oriented: Tell me about a time when you went above and beyond to help a patient or customer.

  In general, you are looking for the following pieces of information for each question:

- What was the situation?
- What did the candidate do?
- What was the outcome?

Continue to ask until you get all three important pieces of information for each scenario.

- **Allow silence so that they have time to think:** If they begin to appear stressed during the silence reassure them that it is fine to take a minute to think of an example. If they still cannot think of one tell them that you will come back to the question at the end.

Stay Away From Illegal or Inappropriate Questions or Topics

- Do Not Ask About Marital Status

  o Not even, "What is your maiden name?" You can ask, "What is your full name?"

- Do Not Ask About children or plans to have a family
- Do Not Ask About religion, race, where they are from, family, age

  o You can ask if someone is 18 years or older if this is a job requirement but cannot ask, "How old are you?"

- Do Not Ask About disabilities or physical or mental conditions.

  o You CAN ask – "Are you able to perform the duties

of this job with our without accommodation?" If there is a disability, they can disclose it and ask for a reasonable accommodation that would allow them to fulfill the job duties.

- Do Not Ask About where someone is a citizen.

  o You can ask if they are legally eligible to work in the United States.

- Do Not Ask About a crime that is not relevant to the job

  o You cannot consider a crime unless it directly affects the ability to do the job. Example: Pharmacists cannot have any drug conviction; Bank tellers cannot have any convictions for theft.

- Do Not Ask whether they have a car.

  o You can ask if there are any reasons why they may not be able to get to work on time each day. That is relevant to the job. You don't care HOW they will get to work.

Stick only to questions relevant to the job and you should be okay!

Control the Interview: Do not let candidates hijack the interview. Keep on topic and stop them if answers get too long, wordy, or off track.

Seek Contrary Evidence: It is human nature to create a first impression. However, this impression is just your gut reaction. You don't want to rely only on this. If you have a good or bad first impression, look for contrary evidence to ensure that you are open and looking for all valid information, not just information that supports your initial reaction.

Give Information about the Job: Include the following information:

- Expectations
- Pay range
- Benefits
- Work schedules
- Work environment

Be as precise and honest as possible. This is your first chance to give them a clear picture of all that the job entails. You don't want to bring in a new employee with a false sense of the job. You want their decision based on as much information as possible. Remember, a good interview process is about finding a great fit not just a warm body! And accurate expectations of the job will help drive their satisfaction of the job. They will accept unpleasant parts of the job more easily if they knew about it up front than if you glossed over it during the interview. Help these potential employees stay out of the gap.

At a minimum, include items like the following:

> **The Company:** How long have you been in business? What's great about it? What are the opportunities for growth? What is your mission?

> **The Decision Process:** When can they expect to hear from you? How many more candidates are there?

Next Steps: Will there be other interviews? Will you call if they are not hired?

I also highly recommend that you provide candidates with an accurate description of the culture.

Afterwards, answer any questions that candidates have about the job, company, or interview process.

✺

Reward to Retain

Once you get the right people in place and you have built a solid team around a great culture, you want each member to feel appreciated. You need a good reward system. You do not want to invest in training and hiring only to have your rock stars leave for the clinic down the road.

Right away, you might be thinking, I do not have that much profit margin. I cannot pay my people anymore than I am right now.

Well, before you travel down that path too far, let's do some reality checking on that:

1. If you have the right staff all working well together and functioning as a fired-up, cohesive team you will have better

productivity. You will also free up more time to market and there will be more word of mouth. You will end up with more patients. The combination of these two things means a higher profit margin.

2. You have no idea, at this point, the true cost of your non-performers. And, I guarantee it is greater than you think. Dead weight out, rock stars in, means more cash. Period.

3. Not all rewards are monetary. We are going to talk about other ways of rewarding your staff that do not require a commitment to a bigger paycheck.

Reward Extrinsically

Extrinsic rewards is just a fancy way for saying "rewards from outside." The most obvious form of extrinsic reward is pay. Pay your people. I have a lot of experience with compensation and I can tell you that when it comes to pay, the number one thing is not necessarily to pay the most, though you do need to be in the ballpark. The most important variable is to communicate the compensation plan clearly to others and assure that it is perceived as fair. This is a place where your walk must meet your talk!

It is human nature to fill in the blanks of missing information with assumptions. And I have found that, when it comes to pay, the information holes are filled with assumptions of inequity, favoritism, unfair treatment.

Your best bet is to tell people how you arrive at salaries, when they can expect raises, based on what criteria and then stick to it. Do not share specific pay amounts, just the philosophies behind pay.

The best case scenario is to have pay ranges for each position that are based on paying to the market value for each job. It may not be the most precise way to create your pay ranges, but check out Salary. com. They have a wealth of information and a team of compensation experts that review that data for accuracy.

So many companies have a policy that states that their employees must keep their compensation private. News flash – few do!! Having the rule alone can lead to a lack of trust. Moreover, if you are not following any set guidelines and this has resulted in major inequities, your employees will find out.

Better to create a rhyme or a reason for the way you pay people, tell people what the rules are and then stick to them consistently.

If you find you should be paying more but cannot bring yourself to do it, opt instead for some sort of bonus structure that is based on the revenue of the clinic. That way, you are not locked in to a higher pay structure if the economics of your clinic change.

Take note, though, if you opt for some sort of bonus plan you may need to include that pay in overtime calculations for your hourly employees. Check with a professional if you go this route.

Reward Intrinsically

Intrinsic motivation comes from inside an individual rather than from an external or outside reward, such as money. Motivation comes from the pleasure of performing the task itself or the sense of satisfaction in completing a task. And, if you have hired people who fit your culture and mission, they should get enjoyment from engaging in the journey. They will be fulfilling their own purpose in your clinic. They are living out their passion by working for you.

This is another reason why it is so important to make sure to follow the strategies outlined in the prior chapter about helping every employee see how they participate in your mission. Even the smallest task is important when attached to that greater goal.

Recognition is a form of reward that does not need to cost money. Timely and appropriate recognition like a high five, card, email, or acknowledgement during a team meeting, are simple ways to show appreciation for someone's effort. You could even utilize a positive comment box where co-workers could share appreciation for each other. The comments could be shared at staff meetings. Sometimes praise from peers is especially powerful.

Growth opportunities are another way to reward intrinsically. If your clinic is big enough, allow rock star employees the opportunity to take on additional, fun duties that provide the opportunity to learn new skills. Do you have room for advancement? Giving someone a bigger title or some supervisory duties is a big plus. If possible, though, you want to include some increase in pay along with the additional responsibility.

Reward with Celebration

"There is no sound as sweet as that of your own
name being spoken in recognition" – unknown

Now, pay close attention. I am going to share with you a professional secret from the world of human resources and staff management. A secret so powerful, if you do just this one thing, it will transform your staff and your world.

Celebrate!!!!!!!

Yep, talking about it again. Even a mini-celebration is a reward. It gives your staff the opportunity to acknowledge progress towards their goals and your mission. Again, it does not have to be a big party with food and hats.

- Have a movie with popcorn during lunch or another down time
- Bring in a cake or other goodies to say thanks.

Sports teams celebrate after every play, every shot, every chance they get. Grown men pat each other on the behinds. Celebrations do not have to be big, extravagant parties, although they can be. They can be small and easy to pull off.

You are working to build a solidified team. Celebrating is a way to bring people together. Lock your team with positive memories.

You have all been around a family that is full of dysfunction, I am sure. The entire focus of each person is to one up, be right, or tear down. It is not fun to be around but for some reason these people stay connected. They are locked in kind of negative force of gravity that keeps them solidified no matter how miserable.

You want to create the exact opposite in your clinic. You want to create a solidified team pulled together through positive experiences, positive interactions, lifting each other up. Do not treat recognition or celebration like a limited resource that people must fight and bicker over. Make recognition, appreciation and celebration abundant. Always authentic but always present. You will model it and your staff will follow.

Lift them up; don't beat them up.

When I teach this workshop, I bring "Focus Stones" with me. To let you in on a little secret, they are just decorative rocks. However, if you attach the concept of focus to them they can work magic! I ask each participant to take one focus stone and then encourage them to take extra for any team members not in attendance. I instruct them to keep the stones handy at work. Some people leave them in a jacket pocket, others on a desk or next to their computer. I ask them to think of something to celebrate every time they see or touch the special stone. It just creates a point of focus for positive, a reminder of what is important. You can use anything. I have had clients put rubber bands around their wrists or attach the concept to their watch or a piece of jewelry. It does not matter what the object is. The goal is to have an often present reminder until you have created the new habit. You will be amazed at how transformative it can be to incorporate celebration into your work-life everyday.

Reward with Appreciation & Feedback

The first responsibility of a leader is to define reality.
The last is to say thank you. - Max DePree

I cannot tell you how many times I hear from employees, "We only hear when there's something wrong. They never tell us when we are doing a good job." It's sometimes difficult to focus on the good when it feels like so much is going awry. But you will burn your team out if you don't provide some positive feedback. I always recommend beginning with something positive before you correct. It is a good rule to use to make sure that the good is staying on your radar. Of course, you do not want that to be the only time that you show appreciation. Otherwise, the compliment will automatically signal an imminent reprimand and will no longer feel authentic.

The goal should be to show plenty of appreciation to all so that there is no one feels left out. Backbiting, gossip and sabotage comes when appreciation is seen as a limited resource. Make recognition abundant but authentic.

So many leaders I have worked with want to treat appreciation and acknowledgement as if they are limited resources. This does not create a great culture. I often use the analogy of starving people trapped in a room with a few morsels of food. Each person will fight and claw to get what they need. People do the same thing with acknowledgement. One of our innate desires is to be recognized. When we don't receive it we feel starved.

The truth about gratitude is that the minute you express it, there is another thank you ready and available for use. Thank yous are abundant and should be shared often.

Make a practice of catching your team members doing something good and let them know immediately. You will find plenty of opportunities.

Another great strategy is to schedule individual time with you, either a lunch or a meeting, to give individual team members the time to talk and bond with their leader. Obviously, the size of your staff is a factor in how often you can meet individually or whether it's even realistic. If you have a very large team perhaps you can spend time with one department at a time. Either way, it will give your team the chance to let you know how they are feeling and what is going on in the office. It will also give you one more opportunity to express your gratitude for a job well done.

Here are some ideas for how to celebrate and show your appreciation, some big and some small, some public, some private.

- Pat on the back
- Send a note
- Give praise in a meeting in front of co-workers
- Say "Great job:
- Say "I appreciate you."
- Give a thumbs up
- Send an email
- Give a gift card
- Provide a catered lunch
- Use a Wow Board (bulletin board with letters of appreciation from co-workers or patients)
- Let someone choose the office music for the day
- Allow someone an extra hour of sleep
- Give someone a special button to wear for the day or week

- Have a pizza party
- Buy some balloons
- Ask employees what would be meaningful to them

Reward with Fulfilling Work and a Great Environment

The beauty of this last section is that if you have done the work outlined in this book along the way the result is fulfilling work and a great environment. You have done it. This is the end reward for you *AND* your team!

The ultimate is to do work you love. On the bio on my Facebook page I say, "My work is play and I love it that way!" My hope is that you will be able to proudly proclaim the same, and mean it!

How awesome if you have gotten to the point where you enjoy your work again. I hope that you are forging ahead towards making your big vision happen, waking up fired up ready to start your day, that you and your team are fulfilling your life's purpose together.

If you are still in transition, keep at it. You are on your way. If you keep taking the methodical steps spelled out in this book it *will* happen. If you need additional motivation or some more convincing, visit my website and click on the testimonials page. You will see many stories from clients who were probably where you are now at one point or another. Go to www.FocusForwardCoaching.com or contact me.

Will every day be perfect? No. However, you will have the tenacity to work through the days that aren't with a clear focus on the prize.

And as your team transforms they will be helping you each step of the way. They will be working, effective extensions of you and your work.

Continue your important work and congratulations on the progress you have made! Take that moment to celebrate now.

And, as I sign every newsletter; wishing you a life of joy, balance, passion and purpose ~ Kirsten

Afterward

On a scale of 1 to 10 how would your rate your success in moving forward and sticking to your commitments? Are you frustrated or energized? Enlightened or discouraged?

If you did not follow through on all that you know you need to, there is no value in beating yourself up. Give yourself grace, make an intentional choice to keep going and move forward. What will you do next?

Do you need additional support to make your vision a reality?

Visit Kirsten's websites and social media platforms to find additional resources or contact her to receive personal assistance:

Website: www.FocusForwardCoaching.com

Membership Site: www.DramaFreeWork.com

Facebook Fan Page: www.Facebook.com/dramafreework

Twitter: www.Twitter.com/dramafreework

Youtube: www.Youtube.com/user/KirstenERoss

Contact Email: KRoss@FocusForwardCoaching.com

Phone: 586.558.6683

Visit www.FocusForwardCoaching.com to sign up for your free newsletter and to purchase the coordinating Catapult Task Workbook and forms download. **Use discount code 12577.**

<u>Catapult Task:</u> **The Final Commitments**

I want a practice wired for passion and commit to making the changes necessary to make it happen.

My Personal Barriers are:

I commit to taking these steps to correct my personal barriers *(Start big or start small. Just get moving!):*

My Office barriers are *(process, patient flow, scripting, marketing, staff, training, consistent consequences, celebrating)*:

I commit to taking these steps to work around my office barriers *(Start big or start small. Just get moving!):*

I commit to the following to add celebration to my practice this week:

I commit to the following to convene my remarkable team:

I commit to keeping my eye on the prize and walking methodically step by step towards my vision. I am a steward of my gifts and have great value to add to the world!

Acknowledgements

I must say that writing a book has been a much more daunting task than I had originally imagined. Getting the first draft complete, to my surprise, was just the tip of the iceberg. That feat itself was such an exercise in tenacity. I had to move through doubt and fear, and carve out the time from a very busy schedule. There are so many people who helped me along the way. I am so grateful for their wisdom, friendship and encouragement. My heartfelt thanks go out to:

Susan Wright for her gentle reassurance that the presentation I described to her was, in fact, the book that I had been envisioning. She encouraged me along the way and helped me with the difficult task of finding a suitable title. Her enthusiastic response to seeing the completed manuscript was much appreciated as well.

Thank you to Lauren Rollheiser, my one link to the industry, who edited my first draft with such care. She brought my words to life while maintaining my voice. She encouraged me to keep going and enthusiastically quipped that I had the tenacity and the skill to get it done – "just go do it!" She gave me the confidence I needed to forge ahead in the early days of the project.

Vicki Vogel was the first person close to me to read the book in its draft form. Her enthusiastic response was well-timed and much appreciated by a writer who had never taken on a project so large.

Jill Jessen has been a blessing. Her attention to detail, knowledge of the English language and demonstrated self discipline have been a true God send.

Andrea McKenzie for her encouragement, enthusiasm and wonderful creativity. I have had the privilege of calling her a friend for years. She is also a talented photographer who has taken tremendous photos for me professionally and personally. She took the pictures that grace my book cover. Her website is: http://andreamckenziephotography.com/

Dr. Rosemary Batajnski for her friendship and encouragement and for her introduction into the world of chiropractic. I have rented space in her office for years and worked on this book in my little corner office there. She has a wonderful passion for her patients and a desire to be her best in all aspects of her life. It has been a privilege to know her and work with her.

Without Dr. Gilling as a catalyst, this all might still be in my head! He invited me to speak at his boot camp for chiropractors. It was that presentation that become the first outline for the book.

Dr. Bala Pai, Senior Associate Medical Director for Health Alliance Plan, a long time friend, who has known me through what seems several life times. Thank you for his offer to assist with getting the word out about my book and for his reinforcement that what I was writing was so necessary. It was very encouraging as I worked to finish the first draft.

Eric Vogel, my encourager and supporter. The calm beside me. He is such a great model of passion in balance. He has a zest for life but knows when it is time to slow down and rest, take in good nourishing food, listen to your body. He is also a tremendous social media consultant who has helped me brand myself and my business. He has been an invaluable resource and I am very fortunate to have him in my life personally and professionally!

Gino Wickman for his clarity, inspiration and energy. It has been a privilege working with many of his clients over the years. He saw the fire in me and gave me the opportunity to use my passions to unleash the leaders in others.

Eric and Daniel, my two boys, are the motivation for all that I do. As a single mom to them my goal has always been to find a great balance so that we are secure financially but also have time to spend together. The years go too quickly and I truly believe that we must put intentional focus on that time together or it will be lost. Thank you to them for their generous spirits, their kind nature their sense of humor, their zest for life, their passion for hobbies, their willingness to learn and grow. They definitely keep me grounded! We have been in it together for years. We are a team!

About the Author

Kirsten E. Ross has a passion for helping leaders with a heart to serve. With a unique blend of energy and insight, Kirsten empowers leaders and improves communication by helping her clients gain self-awareness. Kirsten's approach creates productive and profitable workplaces.

She is a Leadership & HR Coach with a Masters Degree in Human Resource Management with more than 20 years of experience, mostly in health care. She holds a Senior Human Resource Certification and has completed the Coach Training Alliance curriculum. In addition, she has authored a variety of articles and books and has been interviewed as an expert for media outlets such as **NBC Nightly News, Fox 2 News, and National Public Radio** and for publications such as ***Working Mother Magazine*** and ***Fitness Magazine***.

Kirsten is an experienced speaker who adds inspiration and fun to her events, infusing humor and self-awareness activities that keep audiences engaged. Participants leave with individualized strategies that can be implemented immediately to create positive change.

Contact her for your event at: Kross@FocusForwardCoaching.com

Kirsten will help you:

Eliminate Drama in your Workplace

Create Cohesive, Productive Teams

Skyrocket Profits

Enhance Patient Loyalty

Generate "Right Hiring"

Reduce Defensiveness

Decrease Anger & Stress

Improve Communication

Learn more about Focus Forward Coaching and Recruiting and Kirsten's services by visiting: www.FocusForwardCoaching. com

Appendix

Want a full size version of these documents and all of the Catapult tasks? Visit www.FocusForwardCoaching.com products page to purchase the coordinating workbook and forms.
Use discount code 12577

Performance Improvement Plan

Definition: A Performance Improvement (PIP) is a written agreement between an employee and his/her manager that identifies opportunities for growth and the expectations for improvement over a specified period.

Usage: A manager/supervisor will initiate the PIP process when a he or she can document that an employee's performance is below identified expectations.

Sources of documentation can include:

- General policies and procedures
- Disciplinary actions
- Job descriptions
- Performance evaluations
- Customer complaints

The PIP can be initiated at any time and can occur concurrently with a disciplinary action. However, the PIP is an independent process from disciplinary action. The PIP does not affect the progression of the disciplinary process and is not considered a step in that process.

Purpose: To give the employee opportunity to improve performance by establishing measurable criteria, that can be met over a specified period. In addition, the PIP will give the employee opportunity to discuss low performance areas and to understand expectations of the manager/supervisor.

Format: Schedule a meeting with the employee's manager to discuss and review the documented reasons for the plan. Regular performance assessments should be agreed upon and scheduled for the duration of the PIP. A summary sheet is completed and signed by both parties at the final meeting. A copy will be provided for the employee.

Criteria: Criteria are defined as the standard of performance to be met by the employee. The manager, with input from the employee, will determine the standard. All criteria should be measurable and acknowledged by both parties.

The PIP also may include: extra training courses, additional education, and counseling sessions, as deemed necessary for successful job performance.

Accountability: The employee is responsible for reporting to the manager when circumstances impeded his/her ability to complete the guidelines of the PIP.

PERFORMANCE IMPROVEMENT PLAN

Employee Name: _____

Title: _____

Supervisor's Name: _____

Supervisor's Title: _____

Date Reviewed with Employee: _____

This provides a formal Performance Improvement Plan to correct performance in areas that need improvement. To meet the expectations established for your position, you must improve in the specific area(s) noted below and continue successful performance in all other areas.

Performance Improvement Areas:

(*Specific areas which need improvement – use additional sheets where necessary.*)

Performance Improvement Plan:

(*Corrective action to be taken and dates for training, etc. – use additional sheets where necessary.*)

This is to acknowledge that I have, on the date indicated below, discussed the areas of performance in which I need to improve and the corrective action to be taken as indicated by my supervisor. My supervisor has notified me that if my work performance does not improve, it may result in progressive discipline.

My supervisor and I agree to work together to help me improve my performance to a successful level:

Employee's Signature: _____

Date: _____ / _____ / _____

Employee Comments:

Supervisor's Signature: _____

Date: _____ / _____ / _____

Supervisor Comments:

Scheduled Date(s) for Follow-up:

Follow-up Documentation:

Sample Behavioral Based Interviewing Questions

Accountability: Takes responsibility and ownership for one's actions, behaviors, performance, and outcomes.

- Tell me about a time when a project/job was not completed by the deadline, what did you do?
- Tell me about a time when you were asked to do something not in your job description, what did you do?

Communication: Presents ideas clearly and effectively to individuals, orally or in written form, with correct grammar, language, and terminology.

- Describe a time when it was necessary for you to communicate negative information to a patient/customer. How did the customer react? What was your response/action?
- Think of a time when miscommunication occurred between you and _____, after you had time to evaluate the situation, what would you have done differently?
- Describe a time when you suggested a process to your supervisor and it was not accepted or implemented. How did you handle it?

Confidence: Holding the belief that one will act in a proper or effective way.

- Tell me about performance evaluations you have had in the past, highlighting positives and negatives.
- Give me an example of what you consider a job well done.

- Are you comfortable approaching co-workers for input to a problem or do you take a different route to get the answer? Tell me about a specific instance when you had a problem.
- Describe your reaction when your supervisor has asked for clarification of your actions regarding the solution of a problem. Give me a specific example. What was the situation? What did you do?

Courtesy: Consideration, thoughtfulness and respect expressed through specific behaviors.

- Describe for me your principles related to hospitality.
- What does customer service mean to you?
- Tell me about a time when you went out of your way with a thoughtful gesture for a co-worker or patient/customer.

Empathy: Possessing the ability to put oneself emotionally into the other person's shoes, to feel what others are feeling.

- Has there ever been a time that you showed empathy to a patient/co-worker/customer? What were the circumstances and what did you do?
- Can you think of a time when you anticipated a customer's needs before they requested services? What was the situation and how did you handle it? How did the customer react and how did it make you feel?
- What qualities do you think you must have to be successful in this position?

Flexibility: Possessing the ability to maintain effectiveness in varying environments, with different tasks, responsibilities, and people.

- Give me an example of when you demonstrated flexibility in your work assignments.
- Have you volunteered to assist another department or a co-worker with their work assignments or special assignments? What did you do and how did they benefit from your assistance?

Friendliness: Showing interest, a willingness to extend oneself, presenting a positive attitude or demeanor; for example, tone of voice, facial expression, and posture, reflect positive attitude and approachability.

- Tell me about a time when you exceeded a customer's expectations in providing friendly and courteous services. When did it occur and what were the circumstances?
- Think about a time when you went out of your way to assist a patient/visitor who appeared to be lost.

Handles Stress: An individual who can maintain performance while under pressure and/or against opposition, someone who relieves stress in a manner acceptable to himself, others, and the organization.

- Describe for me a stressful situation in your current position. Tell me what happened and how did you handle it?
- Describe a situation when you had to deal with an irate customer. Tell my how you handled that situation.
- Tell me about a time when you were having a stressful day. What were the circumstances and how did you handle it?

Initiative: Asserting one's influence over events to achieve goals; self-starting rather than accepting passively; taking action to achieve goals beyond what is required; being proactive.

- Tell me about a recommendation you made to improve a work process. What were the circumstances and how did it affect your work?
- Describe a time when a customer appeared confused. What did you do?
- Can you tell me about a time you saw a co-worker looking overwhelmed or frustrated? What did you do?
- Tell me about a time when there was a crisis or issue at work. What were the circumstances and what did you do?

Motivated: The extent to which job activities and responsibilities, the organization's mode of operation and values, and the community in which the individual will live and work are consistent with the type of environment that provides personal satisfaction; the degree to which the work itself is personally satisfying.

- Give me an example of a new project implemented by your current or previous employer. What was your role in that project?
- Describe for me how you prioritize your daily work.
- Tell me about a time when you saw a problem at work. What did you do?
- Tell me about a time when you had to overcome a challenge.

Professionalism: The ability to conduct oneself competently and with adherence to quality.

- Give me an example of how you have handled a co-worker

requesting personal information about another co-worker/supervisor.

- Can you tell me about a time when someone who was angry, like a co-worker, confronted you? What was the circumstance and how did you handle it?
- The phone is ringing, you have three patients standing in front of you – what do you do?
- In your previous job, how did you answer the telephone?
- What is the initial conversation that you have when you walk into a patient's room? Run through a scenario.

Problem-Solving: Securing relevant information and identifying key issues and relationships from a base of information; relating and comparing data from different sources; identifying cause-effect relationships and developing a plan; implementing a course of action and evaluating the results.

- Describe steps you have taken when confronted with an urgent question/issue for a supervisor when he or she is unavailable.
- Describe the strategy you use upon encountering a problem.
- Describe a time when you went beyond your specific job description to resolve a patient problem.
- Give me an example of how you have handled a situation with an angry customer/patient.

Responsiveness: Taking action that indicates a consideration for the feelings and needs of others; being aware of the impact of one's own behavior on others.

- Do you recall a time when you went beyond the call of duty?

What were the circumstances, what did you do, and what was the outcome?

- Describe a time when you went the extra mile for a customer. What were the circumstances and what did you do?
- Everyone has had a bad day. Can you think of a time when you were having a bad day? How did it affect your work?
- When a work process was not going smoothly, what did you do? Tell me about a specific time you can think of.

Respect: To consider the differences, opinions, beliefs, and actions of others, without judgment or breech of trust.

- What things do you normally say when ending a phone conversation or encounter with a patient/customer?
- How have you handled a situation in which a co-worker asked you confidential information about a patient?
- How have you handled situations in which customers/patients have been unable to communicate in English?
- Describe the strategy that you use upon encountering a patient complaint. Please be specific.
- What is your response to recognition of a co-worker for excellence in their job?

Team Orientation: Active participation in, and facilitation of, team effectiveness; taking action that demonstrates consideration for the feelings and needs of others; being aware of the effect of one's behavior on others.

- What factors contribute to the success of a department?
- Give me an example of a time when you went beyond the call of duty in your job in a past or current position. What

were the circumstances, what did you do? What was the outcome?

- Give me an example of a time you were asked to do something that was not part of your job. Tell me how you handled it.

Interim Progress Discussion Form

Performance Communication

Interim Progress Discussion

Employee Name: _____

Date: _____/_____/_____

Your informal discussion is scheduled for _____ a.m./p.m. on_____

The purpose of this discussion is to encourage ongoing communication between the supervisor and the employee throughout the year. These questions are provided to assist the discussion process. You are free to use other questions related to your job if you desire.

DISCUSSION QUESTIONS:

1. What has gone particularly well for you, since our last discussion?

2. What has been your most significant accomplishment or contribution since our last discussion?

3. Were there any obstacles that you overcame that made you feel especially proud?

4. In the past four months what parts of your job do you feel you could have performed better?

5. What have you learned in the past four months that will be helpful in the future?

6. Are there any aspects of your job in which you feel you need more education or training?

7. Do you feel that you have the tools and resources to do your job to the best of your ability? If not, please describe:

8. How could I assist you in the future to help you be more effective or do a better job? What could I change to be more helpful to you? What should I continue doing?

9. What suggestions, ideas, or concerns do you have for yourself or about the department?

10. Are there any additional issues you would like to discuss?

Sample Progressive Discipline Form

Progressive Discipline Form

Employee: _____

Job Title: _____

Supervisor or other Complete Care Rep: _____

_____

Current Action		Prior Action	Date
Corrective Action Notice			
Written Warning	Level:	1st Written Warning	
Suspension	Return Date:	2nd Written Warning	
With Pay			
Without Pay			
Termination		3rd Written Warning	
Other			

Details: (Who, What, When, Why, How, Where)

_____

_____

_____

_____

Correction(s) Required of Individual

_____

_____

_____

_____

Deadlines for Action and/or Completion:

_____

_____

_____

_____

Scheduled Follow-Up Meetings:

_____

_____

_____

_____

Action if issue is not corrected	Suspension	Termination	Other

Employee Comments:

_____

_____

_____

_____

Signatures (Signature acknowledges that the issue has been discussed and does not represent agreement)

Supervisor: _____

Date:_____

Employee: _____

Date:_____

Gripe and Grumble Form

(There is room to add your own logo while fitting two to a page)

Turn a Gripe or a Grumble into a Request or a Solution

It's easy to complain, gripe or grumble. But it takes energy without getting you anywhere. And you end up sucking energy from those around you.

If your gripe or grumble is worth spending any energy on then it's worth a bit of time and energy to fix it. If it's not worth your energy to fix it then it's not worth your energy to gripe about.

If you have a gripe or grumble that is worthy, fill out the form, come up with a solution or request and give it to the office manager. Either way, get it off your chest!

Gripe/Grumble:

Request/Solution:

Turn a Gripe or a Grumble into a Request or a Solution

It's easy to complain, gripe or grumble. But it takes energy without getting you anywhere. And you end up sucking energy from those around you.

If your gripe or grumble is worth spending any energy on then it's worth a bit of time and energy to fix it. If it's not worth your energy to fix it then it's not worth your energy to gripe about.

If you have a gripe or grumble that is worthy, fill out the form, come up with a solution or request and give it to the office manager. Either way, get it off your chest!

Gripe/Grumble

Request/Solution:

References

Buckingham, Marcus; <u>Go Put Your Strengths to Work</u>: Free Press; 1 edition (March 6, 2007)

Hawkins, David R.; <u>Power vs. Force: The Hidden Determinants of Human Behavior</u>: Hay House, 2002

Katie, Byron & Mitchell, Stephen; <u>Loving What Is: Four Questions That Can Change Your Life</u>; Three Rivers Press (December 23, 2003)

Lembert, Paul, Be Unreasonable: The Unconventional Way to Extraordinary Business Results, McGraw-Hill; 1 edition (April 25, 2007)

Loehr, Jim and Schwartz, Tony: <u>The Power of Full Engagement: Managing Energy, Not Time, Is the Key to High Performance and Personal Renewal</u>; Free Press (December 21, 2004)

Nomura, Catherine, Waller, Julia & Waller, Shannon; <u>Unique Ability: Creating the Life You Want</u> : The Strategic Coach Inc. (December 1, 2003)

Wickman, Gino. <u>Traction: Get a Grip on Your Business</u>: Gino Wickman